"Coyle's presentation of an alternative image of Mary challenges our traditional Marian devotion and enables us to anchor that devotion on a firm theological basis. The format of Coyle's book makes it suitable not only for meditative reading but also for use as a text for courses in Marian theology in colleges and seminaries.

"However it is used, this book will prove valuable to any reader who seeks a contemporary understanding of Mary, for it allows us to retrieve her as a genuine woman disciple who did not hesitate to proclaim God's concern for the oppressed of this world."

Virginia Fabella, M.M.
Academic Dean
Institute of Formation and Religious Studies, Manila

"Via an inspiring presentation of Mary's participation in the reign of God and a fresh look at the Marian dogmas, followed by a survey of Marian devotion throughout the centuries, culminating in Vatican II and later developments, Kathleen Coyle leads us to a critique of traditional Marian symbols and the presentation of an alternative Marian theology. We move from a submissive image of Mary to that of a strong and resourceful woman who can be our model of discipleship. Warmly recommended to all who search for a mature Marian devotion in a mature Christian life, proclaiming God's liberating message in today's world."

Herman Hendrickx, CICM
Professor of New Testament
Maryhill School of Theology, Manila

"Kathleen Coyle here offers an eminently readable and well-researched overview of biblical and traditional Marian themes. She reviews the development of magisterial teachings and describes predominant symbols, popular devotion, and accounts of Marian apparitions with ecumenical sensitivity.

"*Mary in the Christian Tradition* makes a commendable use of scripture, history, and contemporary scholarship as it proposes an image of Mary who is model disciple, vibrant woman, and friend of the poor and disenfranchised. Coyle handles current theological conversation and controversy deftly and directly while maintaining a moderate feminist-liberationist perspective."

Pamela Smith, SS.C.M.
Author of *WomanStory* and *Womangifts*

"*Mary in the Christian Tradition* is an engaging book, a welcome addition to Marian studies, formal or informal. It offers us a solid historical context for the role of Mary in tradition, while it also lives up to the promise of its subtitle: *From a Contemporary Perspective.* For undergraduate students especially, this balance of history and relevance makes the work attractive. Those of us who teach cannot assume that our students are knowledgeable about the origins of Marian devotion and dogmas. (How often do they confuse "virgin birth" and "Immaculate Conception"?) Yet, our efforts to demonstrate clearly what Mary's role might be today fall short without some historical context. Kathleen Coyle supplies it concisely and concretely.

Denise Lardner Carmody
Bernard Hanley Professor of Religious Studies
Santa Clara University

"Kathleen Coyle writes with great clarity and theological precision. Particularly stimulating are her chapters on the Marian dogmas where she presents the development of these dogmas in the light of contemporary research. Her strength is in a strong and balanced feminist theology measured against traditional information about Mary.

"She affirms whatever is sound and appropriate in the Marian tradition and enlightens the reader and student to those areas that need clarification, correction, or updating."

Bert Buby, S.M.
International Marian Research Institute
University of Dayton

Mary
in the
Christian
Tradition

From a Contemporary Perspective

Kathleen Coyle

Gracewing.

☷
TWENTY-THIRD PUBLICATIONS
Mystic, CT 06355

Revised, North American Edition 1996

Originally published under the same title by Claretian Publications, Quezon City, Philippines, © 1993.

Published simultaneously:
Gracewing House
#2 Southern Avenue
Leominster, Herefordshire HR6 0QF
England

ISBN 0-85244-380-3

Twenty-Third Publications
185 Willow Street
P.O. Box 180
Mystic, CT 06355
(860) 536-2611
800-321-0411

ISBN 0-89622-672-7
Library of Congress Catalog Card Number 95-78539

Printed in the U.S.A.

DEDICATION

For Thomas Swiss and Brigid Coyle Swiss
in gratitude for their witness, their wisdom,
and their many welcomes.

Acknowledgments

A special word of thanks to my brother Neil, and sisters Peg and Grace for the celebrations and the sharing, as together we continue to maintain the well.

My thanks to nephews and nieces, Owen, Katie, Danny, Jackie, and Joanne Coyle with delight and much love, and to Grainne Griffin for her insights and enthusiasm.

Preface

to the Second Edition

The first edition of this book was written in response to the needs of my theology students in Manila, in the East Asian Pastoral Institute, Maryhill School of Theology, and the Institute of Formation and Religious Studies, as well as for the students of Christ the King Seminary, Karachi. Both the Philippines and Pakistan have a strong tradition of devotion to Mary, the Mother of God, and courses on marian theology are included in the theology curricula for men and women preparing for ministry. With the exception of scholarly journals and pious pamphlets, there is a dearth of suitable course material for students.

Like the first edition this second edition hopes to provide material not easily accessible to teachers and students of theology and religious education. This second edition greatly enlarges and revises the first. There is an added chapter on the marian dogmas. The ancient dogmas of Mary's motherhood and the virginal conception of Jesus are treated in Chapter Two while the recent dogmas, the immaculate conception and Mary's assumption, are dealt with in Chapter Three. Chapter Six, "The Tradition of Marian Symbols," and Chapter Seven, "Toward an Alternative Marian Theology," have been mostly rewritten and contain the study of more recent research.

While this book was originally written with Pakistan and the Philippines specifically in mind, I hope this edition provides course material for students of theology beyond the borders of Asia, for together we all share a common Christian heritage.

For the theological insights in this book, I am greatly indebted to Elizabeth Johnson and Anne Carr for their ongoing efforts to define Mary for us today. For the reflection on the Trinity in Chapter Seven, I have availed of the creative and engaging insights of Elizabeth Johnson's *She Who Is: The Mystery of God in Feminist Theological Discourse* and Catherine Mowry LaCugna's *God for Us: The Trinity and Christian Life.* I have made extensive use of the work of these authors and I hope I have acknowledged them adequately.

CONTENTS

Mary in the Christian Tradition

THE INFLUENCE OF MARY IN THE CHRISTIAN TRADITION

Mary very early on became a figure of veneration in the Christian community, and the cult of Mary has grown enormously through the centuries. Devotion to her has become central to the spirituality and art of the Catholic and Orthodox traditions. As early as the year 150 CE a fresco of the virgin and child had been painted in the catacomb of Priscilla in Rome.[1] Prayers, hymns, devotions, and feasts have been composed in her honor. Churches, cathedrals, religious orders, confraternities, and even holy years have been named after her. Her litany addresses her and celebrates her under a variety of names: Virgin, Mother, Madonna, and Queen of Heaven. Thanking God for her and praying for her intercession is an abiding and deeply rooted characteristic of the Catholic community.

The Presence of Mary in the Christian Tradition

Mary has figured prominently in Eastern and Western iconography, inspiring the work of such great artists as Fra Angelico, Leonardo da Vinci, Botticelli, and Raphael. Her frequent portrayal in Christian art gives witness to a deep love for the Mother of God that transcends its theological expression. Stained glass windows, statues, and paintings depict her beauty, as do magnificent cathedrals like Notre Dame de Reims and Chartres, which were built in her honor. Hundreds of Russian icons present Mary as vivid and dark faced, dear to the people's psyche. They portray her as vital, strong, and independent, as well as tender and compassionate. She continues to live in the Catholic soul, in Christian memory and culture, where her stories and legends evoke a tender presence. This is a culture that has often otherwise been experienced as dominating and controlling.

Mary in the Imagination of Christians

At present there is no coherent theology of Mary as a whole. She has remained a religious symbol of enduring power in Christian imagination, yet she is an ambiguous symbol especially for women, for the passive virtues of submission, humility, and docility have been projected on to her. A distinction has to be made between the Mary of the gospels and Mary of the fictional stories that have grown up about her in a devotional tradition. She needs to be liberated from some of the images into which she has been formed. Following Mary as she is often depicted by tradition may deter rather than challenge the radical living out of the gospel. John McKenzie believes that the lack of historical evidence about Mary in the gospels "has left the imagination of Christian devotion entirely unrestrained by information."[2]

Some contemporary images of Mary also do her a disservice. The plaster statues and pictures of her in some of our churches do not represent the strong woman of Nazareth who answered God's call. More often, they present her as meek, timid, deferential, and demure, with eyes downcast, and resigned expression, an image often held as a model of piety for both women and men.

Marian References in Scripture

If the essence of Catholicism has included a strong presence of Mary for almost two thousand years, we may be surprised to discover that there is very little information about her in Scripture. Paul doesn't even mention her name! Luke and Matthew mention her but mostly in the infancy narratives in chapters 1 and 2 of their respective gospels. These narratives cannot be considered historical accounts in the sense that the rest of their gospels are considered historical. In the Acts of the Apostles (1:14) Luke explicitly names Mary among the first believers assembled at Jerusalem, awaiting the coming of the Holy Spirit. John gives prominence to her. His gospel, however, is to be appreciated as a theological reflection rather than a narrative account of the life of Jesus. Finally, the Didache, the so-called teaching of the twelve apostles in the early Christian community, makes no mention of her name. How then has she built up a strong repertoire of roles through the centuries?

Contemporary Ecumenical Interest

The ecumenical spirit of recent years has encouraged Christians to try to understand and appreciate one another's traditions so that they might find in Mary resources for reconciliation rather than conflict. John McKenzie notes that if the free and open ecumenical and theological discussions on Mary that are taking place now had been possible four hundred and fifty years ago, then the Protestant Reformation need not have happened.[3] The collaborative studies by scholarly members of the Lutheran-Roman Catholic ecumenical dialogue are one such effort. These studies were published in *Mary in the New Testament*,[4] and were edited by Raymond Brown et al. in 1978. John Macquarrie's book, *Mary for All Christians*,[5] published in 1991, is another contribution. It began as a series of papers for the Ecumenical Society of the Blessed Virgin Mary, in England, and dates back to 1970.

The Scope of This Book

Chapter One discusses Mary's participation in bringing about the kingdom of God, as well as her prophetic influence for our times. It offers a reading of the scriptural texts that envision Mary as actively responsive to God's call. It critiques interpretations that present her as passively submissive to God's will, interpretations that have functioned to legitimate rather than challenge the oppression of women. Chapters Two and Three take up the study of the marian dogmas. They focus on their evolution, scriptural roots, historical conditioning, and theological significance. They also emphasize the importance of continually contemplating their meaning for the faith life of the Christian community. Chapter Two examines the two ancient and major dogmas: the divine motherhood and Mary's virginity, while Chapter Three deals with the two modern marian dogmas: Mary's immaculate conception and her assumption into heaven.

Chapter Four offers a historical overview of the different images of Mary that have emerged throughout the centuries. It shows how each age unconsciously formed its image of Mary according to its own ideal. This image often tells us more about the church in any particular period in history than about the Mary of the gospels. The breakthrough contribution of Vatican II and the council's efforts to place Mary within the context of the mystery of Christ and the church are discussed in Chapter Five. The commitment of the conciliar fathers to stress the sole mediatorship of Christ and to diminish the marian excesses of former centuries is also discussed. Finally, the contributions of the postconciliar documents that offer "a new and more careful reading of what the council said about Mary"[6] are also addressed.

Chapter Six discusses the long tradition of marian symbols that have captured the Christian imagination both in popular piety and theological reflection. A critique of the Mary–New Eve, and New Adam–New Eve symbols, as well as their influence on the lives of women, is offered. Finally, Chapter Seven shows that an underdeveloped theology of the Trinity and the Holy Spirit has led images of Mary to assume the compassionate attributes of God. With feminist theology this study claims that when theology retrieves the caring characteristics of God, Mary can then be appreciated as our model disciple, a woman strong and resourceful and our sister in faith who calls us to proclaim the liberating message of the Magnificat for the poor of our world.

From a pastoral perspective, the Appendix offers a general comment, without looking at cultural connections, on the phenomenon of apparitions and the meaning of pilgrimage in religious traditions. It discusses the liberating message of Our Lady of Guadalupe, as well as the upsurge in marian apparitions in the nineteenth and twentieth centuries, with their millennial prophecies and messages. Finally it recommends that any theological reshaping of the image of Mary must pay attention to the phenomenon of pilgrimage to marian shrines in popular devotion, a phenomenon that often speaks of people's efforts to unite faith and life.

CHAPTER ONE

MARY'S PARTICIPATION
IN THE KINGDOM OF GOD

An understanding of the concept of the kingdom of God is essential for the study of marian theology, for it is in the context of the kingdom of God that we try to understand the images Mary assumes in Scripture and throughout the long history of the Christian tradition. The term "kingdom of God" is an apocalyptic symbol that speaks of God's irruption into history to renew and remake, and finally to redeem the world and all humankind.[1] The term also includes the action of God compassionately redeeming the peoples of history. It therefore has a double focus: the certainty of a future aspect and the equal certainty of the present experience of the kingdom. Its proclamation is the central message of Jesus' preaching. In him the compassionate action of God is present for us in history, God's glory is revealed, and God's will is done.

All four gospels begin the narrative of Jesus' ministry with an encounter with John the Baptist. In the synoptic tradition the Spirit, who has been promised, descends upon Jesus, signifying that the eschatological time of salvation has begun. Having been "led by the Spirit" through prayer, fasting, and temptation in the desert, Jesus returns to the synagogue in Nazareth. There, echoing the message of Isaiah, he proclaims solidarity with the poor, the captives, and the oppressed. He remains faithful to the Spirit through suffering, crucifixion, and death, is raised to glory, and becomes in turn the life-giving Spirit for others.

There is something undefinable and mysterious about God's kingdom. Jesus never defined it, for it is the ultimate mystery. He just said it is *like* a seed. It is a personal, social, cosmic reality, and its starting point is the experience of God's liberating love. This love is concretized in the neighbor. "Say therefore to the Israelites, I am the Lord, and I will free you out from the burden of the Egyptians, and deliver you from slavery to them. I will redeem you..." (Exodus 6:6–7).

The community of disciples who gathered together with the mother of Jesus in Jerusalem awaited the promise of the risen Christ: "But you shall receive power when the Holy Spirit has come upon you" (Acts 1:8). At Pentecost, when the Spirit descended upon them, inspiring boldness to preach the gospel, they initiated a movement that would witness to Jesus' message of unselfish love. Having faith in him meant choosing the values of God's kingdom, for which he lived and died. It was a way of living, of being for others. This faith was a sign and initial realization of the kingdom of God.

The Presence of the Anti-Kingdom

In Israel the notion of the kingdom of God did not develop from a neutral reality. It began in the presence of an anti-kingdom, the tragic reality of oppressed slaves in Egypt, and it was experienced as God's liberating action in the Exodus. It developed amid the resistance of kings and religious leaders and emerged as a utopia in the presence of the anti-kingdom. The kingdom of God is God's liberating action that:

> executes justice for the orphan and the widow, and who loves the strangers, providing them food and clothing. You shall also love the stranger; for you were strangers in the land of Egypt. (Deuteronomy 10:18–19)

The concern for justice and liberation was even sharpened with the coming of the prophets. Amos lashed out at the merchants who could hardly wait for the holy days to pass so that they could return to their fraudulent practices:

> Hear this, you that trample on the needy, and bring to ruin the poor of the land...buying the poor for silver and the needy for a pair of sandals. (Amos 8:4–6)

Isaiah, too, pronounces God's judgment on the administrators of justice:

It is you who have devoured the vineyard; the spoil of the poor is in your houses. What do you mean by crushing my people, by grinding the face of the poor? (Isaiah 3:14–15)

In the postexilic period, Third Isaiah's preaching stresses that true justice is not an otherworldly justice but one worked out in history. For this prophet, fasting means letting the oppressed go free and breaking every yoke.

Is not this the fast that I choose:… Is it not to share your bread with the hungry, and bring the homeless poor into your house; when you see the naked to cover them, and not to hide yourself from your own kin? (Isaiah 58:7)

Like the prophets of Israel and the early church community, we today are called to incarnate the kingdom of God in the presence of the anti-kingdom of oppression, ecological violence, and a collective third world debt of over a trillion dollars. We are confronted with the reality of grinding poverty especially in developing countries, the uprooting of families who are displaced and forced to live in refugee camps, and the brutality of political oppression. In the words of the Asian bishops, these humiliating injustices amount to "a crisis of survival."[2] Whenever bread is broken, the hungry are fed, and oppressive powers are resisted, solidarity with Christ is being forged, and God's kingdom—the eschatological realization of hope that looks forward to one final, once-and-for-all act of liberation—is becoming a reality.

Mary's Participation in Bringing about the Kingdom of God

It is in the midst of these present, depressing realities that Mary becomes our model of compassion. In our efforts to set people free from the power of sin and death, bringing down the powerful from their thrones and lifting up the lowly (Luke 1:52), we aspire to make the kingdom of God a reality in our world. The following texts, one from Paul, one from Luke, and one from John, show us how different New

Testament writers place Mary within the context of the reality of the kingdom of God. These texts are the early church community's different interpretations of the actuality of God's kingdom. They are also a catechesis by, and for, the church telling the story of God's gracious presence to humankind, in the midst of the events of human history.

1. Paul's Letter to the Galatians

The central theme of all Paul's writings is Jesus Christ. In fact his christocentricism is so strong that the expression "in Christ" appears over 150 times in his letters.[3] He has little to say about the words and works of Jesus, as the later gospels do, but rather concentrates on the paschal mysteries of Christ and on humanity's sharing in these mysteries through the death and resurrection of Jesus. His criterion for holiness is to be centered in Christ and his mysteries through faith.

Paul probably wrote his letter to the Galatians around 54 CE. In this letter he is trying to keep the Christian community faithful to the gospel he has preached to them, and he is concerned that they still want to fulfill Jewish prescriptions of the Law, a tradition that continued to be advocated by a conservative faction within the Galatian church.

"Born of a Woman"

Paul is anxious to proclaim to the Galatians that the new creation is now a reality, because God's Son has come in Mary:

> But when the fullness of time had come, God sent his Son, born of a woman, born under the law, in order to redeem those who were under the law so that we might receive adoption as children. (Gal 4:4–5)

The phrase "born of a woman" is a common expression in Judaism to indicate a person's human condition. Mary is certainly the woman mentioned in this passage. Just as Paul has little to say about Jesus and events in his life, he has still less to say when it comes to recalling Jesus' mother: she is simply the woman who brought Jesus into the world.

To appreciate Paul's theology in Galatians 4:4 we have to situate it in the context of the preceding discussion in Galatians where he compares the situation of human beings under the law with that of faith in Christ:

"a person is justified not by works of the law but through faith in Christ Jesus…" (2:16), and again, "the law was our disciplinarian until Christ came, that we might be justified by faith" (3:24). Of importance to Paul is that, in Christ Jesus, we are all children of God through faith (3:26). Galatians 4:4 is also situated within a discussion on the true sons (and daughters) of Abraham (4:1–31), whom he refers to as "children of the promise" (v. 28), "born according to the Spirit" (v. 29).

Under the law, men and women were in an inferior condition. They were like children or minors who were subject to a "custodian" (3:25) and to "guardians and trustees" (4:2). But Jesus was sent by the Father to liberate them from the law and to insure their status as heirs and as offspring of Abraham.[4] It is not just a new age that Jesus comes to inaugurate but a new humankind. Later on in the text, Paul mentions the two sons of Abraham, one by the free woman, Sarah, and one by the slave, Hagar (4:22–24). In this passage, where Sarah is described as model and mother of all believers, he is paving the way for a later presentation of Mary as the mother of all believers.[5] Ivone Gebara and Maria Clara Bingemer reflect theologically on this text:

> The "fullness of time" that the apostle mentions is both end and beginning; it is the end of a journey during which God led God's people, a journey of self revelation, God speaking to the people "in fragmentary and diverse ways"; it is the beginning, of a new state of things in which God takes human flesh and a human face within history, in the midst of a people, of which the woman Mary is the faithful figure.[6]

Jesus' birth in history is the salvific event that enables all, both Jew and Gentile, to become heirs of that inheritance promised to Abraham. The figure of a Jewish woman giving birth to the messiah under the law of Judaism is the sign that God's kingdom has arrived. The mystery of the incarnation of the Son of God in the "fullness of time," is therefore the central axis of history, and it is this "woman" who forms, of her own flesh and blood, "the flesh and blood that will be recognized as the person of God's very self walking on the paths of history."[7]

2. Luke's Infancy Narrative

The third gospel, whose author is popularly known as Luke, is usually dated around 85 CE. This would indicate that his message is addressed to third-generation Christians. Luke himself, though not necessarily a Greek, is most probably a Gentile convert who came to know about Jesus at Antioch in Syria, where, he tells us, the term "Christian" was first used (Acts 11:26). His gospel is studied together with its sequel, the Acts of the Apostles, which shows how Jesus' followers continued his message and mission in the churches that were first formed in Judea, then Samaria, and throughout the Mediterranean world.

Luke places Mary with Jesus' followers in the upper room in Jerusalem praying and awaiting the coming of the Holy Spirit with the rest of the post-Easter community: "All these were constantly devoting themselves to prayer, together with certain women, including Mary the mother of Jesus, as well as his brothers" (Acts 1:14). This is the last time Mary appears in the New Testament after the death of Jesus.

Mary's Cooperation in the Incarnation (Luke 1:26–38)

The foundation of Luke's portrayal of Mary as model disciple is laid in his gospel's infancy narrative. He gives enough information about her to form a definite portrait, and he allows her to speak for herself. His annunciation story is a message of revelation phrased in postresurrectional language. Scholars have unanimously concluded that although the infancy narratives tell the story of Jesus' birth, they were composed only after the story of his ministry, death, and resurrection was already known. The pattern of the angel's announcement of the birth of Jesus has clear antecedents in the births of Isaac and Samson. It is probable that this tradition was already in the community before Luke or Matthew wrote their birth narratives, and that both of them interpreted that tradition differently—Matthew emphasizing the annunciation to Joseph, and Luke the annunciation to Mary.

The angel's words to Mary reecho what the early church has said about Jesus after his resurrection. The angelic message to Mary in Luke 1:28–37 is a rephrasing of the Old Testament promise of Nathan to the House of David (2 Samuel 7:8–16). Raymond Brown points out that the angel's message—"The Holy Spirit will come upon you, and the power of the Most High will overshadow you; therefore the child to be born will be called holy; he will be called Son of God" (Luke 1:35)—takes statements that Christians had already made about Jesus' resurrection—"declared to be *Son of God* with *power* according to the *Spirit* of holiness by resurrection from the dead" (Romans 1:4)—and applies them to Jesus' conception.[8] These key terms from Paul's letter to the Romans also appear in Luke's baptism scene, when the Holy Spirit descends on Jesus, and the voice from heaven designates him as God's Son (Luke 3:22).[9]

The story of the annunciation is often told as if Mary was suddenly surprised by the angel's visit. The overshadowing of God's presence, the *Shekinah* and God's Spirit on this occasion, is more likely the culmination of Mary's constant fidelity to the grace of the Holy Spirit. Finally the Spirit leads her to her consent to the incarnation, which came to fruition in her giving birth to Jesus. This is the fulfillment of the promise made to Abraham and Sarah. God is no longer to be sought in the clouds as the men of Galilee thought (Acts 1:10), but here in the flesh, in a birth, in a grave, in the daily encounters of women and men.

The annunciation story is not about acquiescence but about empowerment. It is about a young woman in a patriarchal society carrying and bringing her child into the world: "the Lord is with you...do not be afraid... you have found favor with God, you will conceive and bear a son...the Son of the Most High...and of his kingdom there will be no end" (Luke 1:28–33). She was probably within her twelfth or thirteenth year, for that was the customary betrothal age for young women.

This passage does not talk about a passively perfect young woman overwhelmed by divine duty, but about a self-possessed poor maiden who finds favor with God and is willing to cooperate with a wild plan of salvation. She is strong enough to risk believing something incredible about herself: "the Lord is with you!" She collaborates decisively, and her choice not only changes the whole of her life but that of humanity as well. She must be envisioned, then, as an autonomous person, responsive and receptive, courageous and creative, intelligent and apostolic. What was unique in Mary was her hearing the word of God and keeping it (Luke 8:21).

Identifying Mary as the handmaid or servant of the Lord (Luke 1:38) would have struck a chord with those who were familiar with the story of the Isaian servant, to whom Yahweh's own Spirit had been given, and who was called to establish justice on earth (Isaiah 42:1). Even the far-off coastlands await his teaching. Mary must have reflected on the fact that the servant's life, having been spent bringing justice to the nations, culminated in a love unto suffering and death. After Jesus' death and resurrection she would have known how the early church had come to understand Jesus as Yahweh's servant (Acts 3:13, 26).

In Mary's cooperation with God's plan of salvation, God's compassion becomes flesh in our world. Since she has made possible this union of God in Christ with all of humankind, no area of human existence, whether physiological or psychological, is left untouched or unaffected by God's grace. Such contemplative realization of God's presence to us helps us to appreciate that we are living in the mystery of God. Such an experience of mystery does not lead to a withdrawal from the world but rather challenges us to participate in the work of bringing about the kingdom of God. It is an invitation to hear the Word of God and live out that Word in compassionate action.

Mary's response to the angel, "Here am I, the servant of the Lord; let it be done with me according to your word" (Luke 1:38), has unfortunately been interpreted as an unreflective reaction to the message of the angel, a passive submission to the will of God, or a childish dependence on God's initiative. She has been praised for living at less than full capacity: "I will do whatever you say!" The Mary of the annunciation story, however, is not paralyzed by timidity. Anne Carr challenges this androcentric bias:

> Thus her theological portrayal as one who is completely passive, obedient...is unacceptable today. Rather we must say that Mary, like the other disciples, received faith in the *active* obedience that is the *receptivity* of Christian faith.[10]

Marina Warner, in her book *Alone of All Her Sex*,[11] holds that such an understanding of Mary—as timid and taking directions from others—helped to define the shape of the feminine ideal for centuries. Warner adds that these traditional images of Mary have often legitimated rather than challenged women's subordination and have functioned to keep them oppressed.

Mary responds to the news of Jesus' conception with the words: "Be it done to me according to your word" (Luke 1:38). To appreciate Luke's message, we have to see it in the context of another Lucan passage, Luke 8:19–21:

> Then his mother and his brothers came to him, but they could not reach him because of the crowd. And he was told, "Your mother and your brothers are standing outside, wanting to see you." But he said to them, "My mother and my brothers are those who hear the word of God and do it."

Luke, knowing Mary's faith response to the word of God, highlights this in the annunciation story. He affirms that Jesus' mother heard the word of God and gave her faithful response to that word during her life. In the words "My mother and my brothers are those who hear the word of God and do it" (v. 21), Luke shows that what Mary does at this moment is consistent with her lifelong courageous faith and strength of commitment.

Mary's Magnificat: Luke 1:46–55

Luke found it fitting to attribute the Magnificat to Mary because she provided a compelling model of discipleship for his community. He portrays her as a woman of action, leaving at once to visit her cousin Elizabeth. This pericope is commonly called the visitation, for it describes the meeting of two women who share the grace of being pregnant with children who will have special missions in God's plan of salvation.

A little imagination will help to fill out the details of Luke's summary account of the visitation story. We need not imagine Mary bursting forth in prophetic praise as she finally arrived, breathless and weary, on Elizabeth's doorstep. It is more probable that, after an animated welcome and the initial excitement of meeting, Elizabeth would sensibly have offered her pregnant and road-weary cousin a meal and a bed.

Mary's haste and Elizabeth's loud cry of praise show the exuberant joy of these two expectant mothers. Both women must have been very conscious of the part they were playing in the history of salvation: Mary preparing to give birth to the Messiah, Elizabeth preparing to give birth to the prophet who would prepare the way for that same Messiah.

In the ensuing weeks both women would have shared their pregnancy experiences and supported each other's journeys in faith. They would also have shared their concerns for Israel. This is the only scene in the entire gospel where two women meet and hold center stage.[12] They were engaged in radical, subversive conversation and prayer that expressed their hope of changing the unjust structures of their society. This could only be achieved by putting down the powerful, raising up the lowly, the poor, and the marginalized of their world, and filling the hungry with good things (Luke 1:52–53). In biblical language, the poor/humble/lowly "is a clear reference to the people of Israel, usually in conditions of domination, oppression, and affliction."[13] Herman Hendrickx[14] suggests that Luke was most likely referring to the urban poor of the city where his community was situated. They now become the recipients of Jesus' good news.

Speaking for the anawim, Mary sings a song of the oppressed in which she and Elizabeth express their concerns for the Israel of their day. Her prophetic speech characterizes God's coming as compassion, the fulfillment of the promise made to Abraham and Sarah. Mary offers a perspective for perseverance and sets a definite agenda of what has to change: the world must be turned upside down. Such a challenge demands faith, and Luke tells us that Mary believed "that there would be a fulfillment of what was spoken to her by the Lord" (Luke 1:45).

As Mary and Elizabeth grew together in intimacy with their God and in inexhaustible compassion for their people, we can imagine that, at a heightened moment of prayer, Mary would have made her own the sentiments and concerns of Hannah after the birth of Samuel (1 Samuel 2:1–10), and sang of these in grateful song. Luke captures these sentiments for us in the Magnificat, which he places as a prelude to Jesus' announcement of his own mission to liberate the poor and marginalized (Luke 4:18–19). And although Mary did not always understand Jesus' mission, she remained faithful to the end, pondering all these things in her heart (Luke 2:51). "Things" has the Hebrew meaning of both words and actions. Mary is like the wise scribe who ponders (see Sirach 39:1–3) in her heart, in the core and depth of her being (Luke 2:19). It takes time to enter contemplatively into truth, and we see Mary here profoundly and reflectively involved in the interpretation of the incarnation event. The tradition of Luke's community recalled the meeting of these two women who had heard the word of God and continued to keep it.

Mary was open to salvation and responded to it. She traveled, perhaps more than most Galilean women of her class. Besides visiting Elizabeth, she accompanied Joseph to the feasts in Jerusalem. She followed Jesus to Capernaum when his opponents and some of his relatives believed he was out of his mind (Mark 3:21, 31; Luke 8:19). She also must have been aware of the conflict between him and his relatives and neighbors long before it climaxed in the confrontation in Nazareth (Luke 4:28–30). Luke presents Mary as committed to the saving work of God made manifest in Jesus.

The gospel portrayal of Mary ends with a final focus on her discipleship. Before the risen Christ "withdrew from them and was carried up into heaven" (Luke 24:51), he said to his disciples: "And see, I am sending upon you what my Father promised; so stay in the city, until you have been clothed with power from on high" (Luke 24:49). And in Acts 1:14 we find Mary with the members of the Jerusalem community, gathered together and awaiting this "power from on high," the gift of the promised Spirit at Pentecost.

Echoing Mary's Magnificat Today

Mary's prophetic speech is echoed in our own time in the words of contemporary theologians and church documents. In his early writings Edward Schillebeeckx emphasizes Mary's role in rearing and educating Jesus:

> His human qualities and character were formed and influenced by his mother's virtues....Mary's function in the Incarnation was not completed when Jesus was born. It was a continuous task, involving the human formation of the young man, as he grew up from infancy to childhood and from childhood to adulthood.[15]

Vatican II sees Mary as a close associate of Jesus throughout his entire redeeming life. This association is described as her "pilgrimage of faith."[16] The 1974 statement *Justice in the World* emphasizes that "action on behalf of justice and participation in the transformation of the world fully appear to us a constitutive dimension of the preaching of the gospel."[17] Paul VI in his apostolic exhortation *Evangelii Nuntiandi* also reminds us that commitment to bringing about the kingdom of God demands of us a faith that is aware and responsible. The pope's letter stresses the importance of the church's critical and transformative activity in the face of unjust structures that dehumanize people:

> for the church it is a question not only of preaching the gospel in ever wider geographic areas or to ever greater numbers of people, but also of affecting and as it were upsetting, through the power of the gospel, humankind's criteria for judgment, determining values, points of interest, lines of thought, sources of inspiration and models of life, which are in contrast with the Word of God and the plan of salvation.[18]

In the ecumenical statement *Mary in the New Testament*, the authors agree that "from the New Testament pictures of Mary we have learned something of what faith and discipleship ought to mean within the family of God."[19]

3. The Fourth Gospel

In contrast to the synoptics, the Gospel according to John offers us a radically different portrayal of Christ. Writing around the end of the first century, the fourth evangelist directs our thoughts to the reality of the incarnation and the divinity of Jesus, the word of God made flesh. After a generation of Christian reflection on the gospel, the author selects the themes that best serve the interests of his teaching. He is concerned about the symbolic potentialities of words and events, and such symbolism must be considered in interpreting the meaning of Christian discipleship. The most important and deeper level of meaning in this gospel concerns the mission of the risen Jesus in the community. The role of Jesus' mother, which we are about to discuss, will therefore be understood in view of her place in the life of the community.

Link between the Cana Sign and the Other Johannine Signs

Scholarship has recognized that Mary's role at Cana cannot be understood by itself, but only in relationship to Jesus' coming hour of death and glory, of which he has just spoken (John 2:4). Joseph Grassi, in his book *Mary, Mother & Disciple: From the Scriptures to the Council of Ephesus*, shows the connection between the Cana sign and the other signs in the gospel.[20] He offers some persuasive arguments from M. Girard, a French exegete, who suggests a restructuring of the principal sign narratives.[21] Girard lists the seven signs as follows:[22]

1. the wedding feast at Cana (Jn 2:1–12);
2. the restoration of the dying son (Jn 4:46–54);
3. the sabbath healing at Bethesda (Jn 5:1–16);
4. the multiplication of the loaves (Jn 6:1–71);
5. the sabbath healing of the blind man (Jn 9:1–41);
6. the restoration of Lazarus to life (Jn 11:1–44);
7. the great hour of Jesus: his mother, the cross, the issue of blood and water from Jesus' side (Jn 19:25–37).

This list excludes the walking on the waters, traditionally listed as one of the seven Johannine signs. Grassi, following Girard, sees this narrative instead as part of the message and meaning of the multiplication of the loaves narrative. He prefers to list Jesus' hour on the cross as the seventh sign and shows that the first six signs are incomplete in themselves and point to this final sign of Jesus' death and glorification. It is through his death and glorification that he will be lifted up and draw everyone to himself (John 12:32). In the following reflection, we will place Mary's role from Cana to Calvary within the above suggested restructuring of the principal sign narratives of the fourth gospel.

Mary, Jesus' Mother at Cana

Jesus, his mother, Mary, and the disciples are present at the wedding feast. The very fact that the mother of Jesus is mentioned in the first verse, which supplies the setting for the miracle, and that she raises the question concerning the wine, clearly directs our attention to her. A wedding feast and banquet is a well-known symbol of the messianic days (Isaiah 25:6; Daniel 5:1; Matthew 22:2).

When the wine runs short, an occasion for public embarrassment, Mary comments on the lack of it, then requests the waiters to "do whatever he tells you" (John 2:5). This message is also for the early church community, who must participate in Jesus' hour and its meaning if they wish to participate in the choice wine of the new age. Jesus refuses to respond to his mother's request because it is not "his hour": it is not yet the real manifestation of his glory (John 17:24). What he wants to accomplish at Cana will only be manifest through the seventh and last sign, on the cross.

The fourth evangelist describes Mary's response to Jesus in such a way that her faith is never in doubt. Without witnessing any miraculous signs, she knows what he will do. She demonstrates that her relationship to Jesus is based on her faith in him, and not merely on their biological relationship. His death, to which the Cana sign points, is a death his mother will witness and remember. We note the parallel to the seventh sign, where Jesus obeys the Father's will and drinks the cup of suffering prepared by his Father. Mary's continuing role within the community is that of a concerned mother, pointing in obedience to Jesus' word, understood now in the light of his death. As intercessor, she continues to request the new wine of the Spirit for the church.

Mary's Presence and Witness to Jesus' Hour

The Cana miracle has set the stage for the evangelist's presentation of Mary at the hour of Jesus' death and glorification. The seventh sign begins with the statement that the mother of Jesus stood by the cross along with the other women (John 19:25). By introducing Mary into the section of the gospel that deals with Jesus' "hour," in which he was departing from this world to the Father, the gospel brings her into the context of discipleship.[23]

In a special scene, Mary and the beloved disciple are the object of Jesus' final instructions. Both are witnesses to the meaning of Jesus' death. His words to his mother, "Woman, behold your son," and to the beloved disciple, "Behold your mother," bear a wide range of symbolic meaning. The beloved disciple is not just being asked to take care of Mary. These words carry a message of revelation for the evangelist's wider audience. The relationship between Mary and the beloved disciple represents the unity of true believers, for which Jesus has earlier prayed: "Holy Father, protect them in your name, that you have given me, so that they may be one, as we are one" (John 17:11).

Mary was not just a witness to Jesus' death. As his mother, his dying on the cross—and the pain she felt—were seared in her memory for the rest of her life. She saw him bow his head as "he gave up his spirit" (John 19:30), a phrase symbolic of the gift of the Spirit to his followers. She witnessed the effects of his death as bringing the promised Spirit to the community, the community of the beloved disciple to which she now becomes a mother. As the one who remembers Jesus' death, she will be a carrier of tradition, and her presence in the community will be a continual reminder to them of his mission and death. Finally, as the preeminent witness of who Jesus is and of how he died, her place in the church will continue to draw its source from his death and resurrection.

Mary, Our Model of Faith

In the vivid scenes of Cana and Calvary we find Mary, "that mysterious figure of autonomy and relationship,"[24] to be our model of faith from unbelief to belief in our slow and often painful growth in faith as we try to discern the "signs of the times" and respond with compassionate action. When we see women and men denied their dignity, many of them working with their emaciated bodies to feed their starving children, when we see the distended stomachs of starving children as they try to live off garbage dumps, when we see all the signs of the anti-kingdom, we are reminded that the cross of Jesus is the historical scandal whereby God identifies with the victims of history. Jesus' hour of his dying, rising, and being glorified proclaims that God is not neutral but takes the side of the "nonpersons" of history. If we are to give the words "Behold your mother" their wide range of symbolic meaning, we must therefore refuse to trivialize tragedy. Because of Mary's permanent association with Jesus in his hour, she continues to remind the community of what his death stood for. Through her symbolic identity with the church, she directs the community to obey his words.

Questions for Reflection and Discussion

1. The call to live prophetically and work for justice and liberation is as urgent today as it was in the time of the Hebrew prophets. How and where do we respond to this call locally and globally?

2. Mary and Elizabeth collaborated decisively with God's plan of salvation. What did that collaboration entail? What does it entail for us today?

3. Both Luke and John present Mary as the model disciple. Discuss this in the context of the themes of their respective gospels.

4. How does the fourth gospel show the intimate connection between Mary's role at Cana and Jesus' coming hour of death and glory?

Suggestions for Further Reading

Buby, Bertrand. *Mary of Galilee: Mary in the New Testament.* New York: Alba House, 1994.

Grassi, Joseph. *Mary, Mother & Disciple.* Wilmington, DE: Michael Glazier, 1988, pp. 9-95.

Hendrickx, Herman. *A Key to the Gospel of Luke.* Quezon City: MST/Claretian Publications, 1992.

McKenzie, John. "The Mother of Jesus in the New Testament," *Concilium* 168, eds. Hans Küng and Jürgen Moltmann. New York: Seabury Press, 1983, pp. 3-11.

Perkins, Pheme. "Mary in Johannine Traditions," *Mary, Woman of Nazareth,* ed. Doris Donnelly. New York: Paulist Press, 1989, pp. 109-122.

CHAPTER TWO

THE MARIAN DOGMAS I

The scriptural reflection in the last chapter focused our attention on Mary, who heard God's word and gave her faithful response to that word by her life. The marian dogmas glorify Mary. She is exalted precisely in her insignificance and simplicity, and it is through the insignificant, the poor—like Mary and those whom Mary declares liberated—that the kingdom becomes a reality among us. Throughout the long history of the Christian tradition the marian dogmas have concentrated our attention on the glory of God shining on the mother of Jesus. In the next two chapters we will study the evolution of these dogmas. This chapter deals with two ancient dogmas, Mary's divine motherhood and her virginity. The immaculate conception and the assumption will be studied in Chapter Three. But first we will say a few words about the development of dogma.

The Evolution of Dogma

The mysteries of faith as expressed in doctrines and dogmas are historically conditioned. Their meaning, therefore, is not always self-evident to those in another historical setting. Dogmatic formulae bear the marks of the philosophical and theological thinking of their time and may not always be the most suitable for every time and place. Their meaning may even change from one historical period to another. As theologians articulate and formulate the meaning of God's incarnation in human history they do so in the context of contemporary societal changes and in light of the church's tradition. It is their task to critically reflect on the experience of faith, taking into account that such experience never exists in a pure state but is always *interpreted* experience, which makes use of the symbols and concepts of a given time and culture. It is thus that the unfolding expression of the church's doctrine is corrected and enriched. It is also the theologians' task to recover an understanding of dogma that has been lost in modern times, namely, that dogmas engage one's entire person—mind, feelings, body—in an existential encounter with truth; otherwise we find ourselves merely repeating formulae.

In their efforts to respond to the tradition that has concentrated on Mary, theologians listen to the movement of the faith community and engage in a search for formulae that give meaning to, and make explicit, the mystery of Mary in the life of the church. In fidelity to that tradition we will sketch the historical development of the marian dogmas and highlight their theological meaning for today.

I. Mary, Mother of God

The title *Theotokos,* "Godbearer" in Greek, was given to Mary at the Council of Ephesus (431), the third ecumenical council of the church. The theme of Mary's divine motherhood runs through the church's earliest councils—Constantinople I (381), Ephesus (431), and Chalcedon (451). The word *Theotokos* consists of two elements: *Theos* (God) and *tokos* (a creature who gives birth). It is not certain who first used the title *Theotokos*. Most probably the term was first used among Egyptian theologians in the fourth century.[1] It was certainly used by Alexander of Alexandria (c. 319).

The Council of Ephesus was summoned to settle a complex controversy between Nestorius, bishop of Constantinople, and Cyril, Patriarch of Alexandria. Nestorius and the Antioch school had become alarmed because the Arians had so exalted Christ that he no longer seemed human. They were therefore concerned that a clear distinction be made between the two natures in Jesus and suggested that Mary should be called, not Mother of God, but "Mother of Christ," "Christbearer" but not "Godbearer." They believed her to be the mother of Jesus' humanity but not of the divine Word. The issue was also aggravated by the tension between the Egyptian church, which supported the title "Mother of God," and the church of Antioch, which supported the title "Mother of Christ."

Nestorius' preaching against the use of the title *Theotokos* for Mary sparked great controversy between oriental bishops in support of Nestorius and Cyril's Alexandrian adherents. The Council of Ephesus stated:

> If anyone does not confess that Emmanuel is truly God, and therefore that the blessed Virgin is truly Mother of God, *Theotokos*, for she bore according to the flesh him who is Word from God, let him be anathema.[2]

The definition was a direct outcome of the controversy over the unity of the two natures in Christ. Ephesus reasoned that if Jesus Christ is God's word incarnate, then she who bore him can be called the Mother of God. The council affirmed that Jesus is one divine person, not two as the Nestorians had argued. Within the one Christ, both Son of God and Son of Man, two natures are conjoined without the suppression of either the divinity or humanity of Christ. Because Christians affirm that the word has become flesh, they declare that the one Christ was born of Mary, suffered and died for us, and is worshiped as Lord. Consequently Mary is truly the Mother of God and not only the mother of the human Jesus. Her divine maternity is understood as concomitant to the mystery of the hypostatic union.

Nestorius' teaching was condemned. Cyril of Alexandria's victory over him and his opponents ensured the success of the cult of Mary, because it emphasized her unique role as the bearer of God.

The West later accepted the title *Theotokos* and qualified it in the creed of Chalcedon in 451. Pope Leo I offered a formula that incorporated Nestorius' concern for a clear distinction between the two natures in Jesus. In the words of the Council of Chalcedon Jesus was "…born of the Virgin Mary…according to his humanity." What the Council of Ephesus had solemnly declared, the Council of Chalcedon spelled out in an explicit dogmatic statement.

The Monophysites, on the other hand, held the view that after the incarnation Christ had only one (divine) nature. In opposition to Nestorius they spoke of Christ's heavenly flesh, the fruit of the work of the Holy Spirit, thus making Mary's motherhood unreal. Against them Chalcedon emphasized Jesus' bodily and human dimension: "the Son born of the Father before all times as to his divinity, [is] born in recent times for us and for our salvation."[3] In stressing the oneness of the word made flesh with all of humanity, Chalcedon asserted that Mary's motherhood was genuine and true.

Scriptural Roots of the Dogma of Mary's Motherhood

The opening chapters of Luke are rich in Old Testament symbolism. Mary is depicted as the new Ark of the Covenant, God's dwelling who journeys to the house of Elizabeth. Just as the Ark of the Covenant was carried from Ba'alejudah to Jerusalem to be received with rejoicing and praise (2 Samuel 6:2–16), so Mary the new ark is greeted by the joyful leaping of the child in her cousin's womb. Elizabeth declares Mary blessed in her motherhood and proclaims her "the Mother of my Lord" (Luke 1:43). The presence of God in the ark, which the people of Israel adored, and to which only the high priest had access, is now, through the mystery of the incarnation, manifest in the face of every human being. From the moment God's word took flesh in Mary, human beings have become God's dwelling place on earth.

Unlike other marian dogmas, Mary's divine motherhood has deep and solid scriptural roots. In the New Testament Mary is referred to as mother no less than twenty-five times, while only two texts refer to her as virgin (Luke 1:27 and Matthew 1:23).[4] As we have seen in Chapter One, Paul, in his letter to the Galatians, speaks of the Son sent by the Father in the fullness of time. This is Mary's Son, who shares the Father's divinity and who begins to exist in her at the moment of the incarnation. The Son who existed from all eternity takes flesh in Mary's flesh and assumes our frail and poor human condition. It is he who gives us the power to call God Father and become God's children. Like him, we too will be raised from the dead by the power of the Holy Spirit.

Mary, the Mother of God, in the Eastern Liturgy

The *Theotokos* is the central marian affirmation of the Eastern church. To a much greater extent than the West, the East celebrates the glory of the *Theotokos* in the liturgy, often with her full title, Our All Holy, Immaculate, Most Blessed and Glorified Lady, Mother of God and Ever-Virgin Mary. At the heart of Eastern spirituality is the glory of the incarnation, with its concern that divine life might irrupt into the world. "In him we see our God made visible and so are caught up in love of the God we cannot see" (Preface of Christmas Liturgy).

In the East's tradition of icons, Mary appears in a privileged place on the iconastasis, the screen in front of the altar that depicts Christ, the angels, the patriarchs, and saints. She stands at the heart of the communion of saints. The most famous icons are those of the *Theotokos*, where Mary holds her Son, the *Deesis*, where she raises her hands in intercession, the *Hodegetria* (pointing the way), where she points to her Son, and the *Eleousa* (Mother of Tenderness), where Mary's eyes look forward to the passion while holding the child to her cheeks.[5]

Mary's Motherhood: Theological Implications

To confess that God has taken flesh like ours, has "emptied himself, taking the form of a servant" (Philippians 2:7), and has joined our human race, is to state that the kingdom of God has arrived in our midst. Mary, in whose womb Jesus came, is the figure and symbol of the new community that experiences this new reality of salvation. God, present in Jesus by means of woman's flesh,[6] is now present especially in the poor and the marginalized of history. In and by the flesh of Mary, God has entered our world fulfilling the prophecy that "all humankind shall see the salvation of our God" (Luke 3:6).

Christianity, however, was nurtured in the world of Hellenistic beliefs. Because of this historical Greek influence, our spirituality has been profoundly influenced by dualistic perceptions. Dualism separates matter and spirit, body and soul, female and male, emotion and reason. Such alienating perceptions of reality identify men with spirit and reason. Women, on the other hand, are strongly identified with body, nature, and sexuality, thus denying them any possibility of representing divinity.

The mystery of the incarnation consistently refuses to accept these ancient dualistic assumptions that fragment life into independently existing parts. As mother of our savior, Mary is concerned for the salvation of the universe that her Son has come to redeem. We therefore resist an alienated, world-fleeing view of redemption that expresses a pessimism toward the world, and which does not appreciate the goodness of God's physical creation. Mary's motherhood, then, is not just the bearing of Jesus' humanity. "It is the birthing of divine power through which the world itself was created."[7]

II. The Virginal Conception of Jesus

Although the church has never offered a dogmatic formulation on the virgin birth, it does consider this belief among its dogmas. The teaching on Mary's virginity and her virginal conception of Jesus states that Jesus was born of the Virgin Mary by the overshadowing of the Holy Spirit without the intervention of a human father.

Paul's letters say nothing about Mary's virginal conception of Jesus. The first gospel and the fourth gospel are also silent on the matter. The infancy narratives of Matthew and Luke are the only sources we have for the virginal conception of Jesus. They testify that Mary conceived Jesus by the power of the overshadowing of the Holy Spirit without male intervention (Luke 1:26–38; Matthew 1:18–25). Scholars caution us, however, that the infancy narrative accounts are not on the same historical level as the narratives that tell us about, for example, the death of Jesus.

The idea that the virgin birth represents a completely miraculous act of God is common to both Matthew and Luke. Their versions differ entirely in detail; the discrepancies in their accounts are in fact irreconcilable. Both authors are interested in the conception of Jesus by his virgin mother as a sign of divine choice and grace. They see his extraordinary birth as a christological insight that Jesus' origin was in God, that he was God's Son and Messiah from birth.[8] Neither evangelist knew the other's infancy narrative, and the fact that a virginal conception through the power of the Holy Spirit is one of the few points on which they agree means that the tradition must have been in circulation long enough to have been well known in their respective communities. In Jesus' miraculous conception:

> The pattern of God's work in salvation is seen in discontinuity amidst continuity. The virginal conception is the miraculous discontinuity while the lineage of David through Joseph is the continuity.[9]

Annunciation Narratives

As we saw in Chapter One, Luke's annunciation narrative contains a post-resurrection proclamation of Christian faith: Mary is being presented as the first to hear the gospel. She does not fully understand the meaning of events, yet she seeks to penetrate their meaning. The angel's annunciation is concerned with the greatness of Jesus and, as we said, is primarily christological. Annunciation stories are standard biblical ways of emphasizing that this person was destined to play a significant role in salvation history.[10] The annunciation of Jesus' birth relates his story to the earlier history of Judaism, which involved similar annunciations. Mary's question, "How can this be since I am a virgin?" (Luke 1:34), may be interpreted, not as Mary's puzzlement, but as a literary device, a standard feature of an annunciation pattern to advance the dialogue and story.[11] It offers the angel a chance to explain that the conception will be virginal. Thus Mary is portrayed in Luke as mother of the Messiah through an extraordinary divine action. His portrait of Mary comes in response to questions arising in the Christian communities, especially Ephesus.[12] Jesus' unusual origin from a virgin is even more remarkable than that of Isaac. Joseph Grassi notes:

> Gnostic-influenced teachings tended to discount history, continuity and the reality of Jesus' humanity, especially in his death and risen presence in the eucharist. Luke presents Jesus' mother as a witness and a guarantee of historical continuity and succession.[13]

Matthew's Infancy Narrative

Matthew, on the other hand, gives us little information about the person and character of Mary. How did he understand Mary's virginal conception? In the rabbinic writings with which Matthew would have been familiar, a "virgin birth" referred to a conception that had taken place before there was any evidence of fertility. The prophet Isaiah's vision of a virgin bringing forth a great king of the Davidic dynasty is a sign of God's presence to his people. Matthew is concerned with the prophetic evidence, with the proof that Jesus really is, according to his origin, the expected Messiah, David's son (Matthew 1:20) and Emmanuel (Matthew 1:23, 25). His focus on Mary's virginal conception of Jesus by the Holy Spirit is his unique way of teaching that Jesus is truly Messiah and Son of God from birth. The image of a virgin-mother and child was an important one for Matthew and his community. This sign is a reminder of a loving God, faithful to God's promises, and inaugurating a new age in the world. The same sign is a reminder of who Jesus is: the unique Son of God, Emmanuel, God-with-us.

The Virginity of Mary: Theological Reflections

The doctrine of Mary's virginal conception begins to take on meaning when contemplatively approached in the context of the incarnation. It points to the mysterious origins of Jesus in God. What is special about him cannot be explained by human parentage alone but is due to God's creative initiative. God's inner mystery has now been revealed in history. The doctrine also points to the future kingdom of God. We witness to its actualization by helping to make it a reality in our world.

With the exception of Tertullian, the majority of scholars from early Christianity to modern times, that is, from the second until the eighteenth century, have accepted the perpetual virginity of Mary in a biological sense.[14] Briefly, they have upheld: Mary conceived Jesus while remaining a virgin; her virginity was not altered by childbirth; she remained a virgin in her marriage to Joseph.

Conceiving Jesus by the overshadowing of the Holy Spirit, without male intervention, *virginitas ante partum,* is affirmed by Scripture. Postbiblical apocryphal literature extended Mary's virginity to include her giving birth to Jesus, *virginitas in partu.* Though not affirmed by Scripture, the patristic church developed the belief that Mary remained a virgin all her life and had no sexual relations with Joseph after the birth of Jesus, *virginitas post partum.* His brothers and sisters (Mark 6:3) are interpreted as cousins or stepbrothers and sisters.[15]

Christianity was unanimous in its conviction that Jesus was conceived virginally, that is, without the involvement of a human father. "For the mass of Christians it was an unexamined doctrine taken for granted."[16] Though long in Christian tradition, the belief that Mary was a virgin before, during, and after the birth of Jesus was given official status only at the Lateran Council in the year 649.[17] It became solemn teaching in the year 1555 with the Constitution, *Cum Quorumdam* of Paul IV.[18]

Today, however, an increasing number of contemporary theologians would not place such emphasis on the physical virginity of Mary. They would be open to the suggestion that there is no reference in the New Testament to Mary remaining a virgin after the birth of Jesus.[19] They are concerned theologically with the fact that Mary's virginity speaks of her holiness, of her being receptive to the Holy Spirit. In the Hebrew Scriptures Israel is called Virgin Israel to symbolize her sacredness. She was set apart from the other nations to be a holy people. Virgin Israel is concerned, not just with this present age but with the age to come. In Mary, the union of Yahweh with Virgin Israel takes place. In Mary too, the holiness of the people is concentrated in one person. Her virginity symbolizes not just her moral virtue, but her holiness, her being set apart from this dehumanized world.

This latter view focuses not so much on the absence of sexual relationships but more importantly on Mary's receptivity to the Holy Spirit. Paul's reference to Isaac, as "born according to the Spirit" (Galatians 4:29) need not imply that he had no human father.[20] In focusing on the theological meaning of Mary's virginity, these contemporary theologians ask if to deny Jesus a human father is not also to deny him the normal and natural development of a human person. Does being human not involve being genetically connected to the prehistory of the human race? Without a human father could Jesus of Nazareth really be human? Without this genetic connection, could he be, as the letter to the Hebrews states, the "one who in every respect has been tested as we are but without sin" (Hebrews 4:15)? The virginal conception therefore need not exclude the fatherhood of Joseph.

Other critics question whether the virgin birth is not an application of familiar religious views from the surrounding cultures to Jesus' mode of birth, a part of an ancient worldview that is clearly out of date. After all, in antiquity many extraordinary persons were considered to be virginally conceived: their origin was thereby divine, and not merely human. Others again have objected that taking the virginal conception literally devalues sexuality and suggests that it would be demeaning for Jesus to have come into the world through the sexual love of a man and a woman.

The Cautious Conclusion of Scholars

Exegetes assert that the virginal conception of Jesus cannot be proven by critical exegetical methods. The cautious conclusion of scholars such as Raymond Brown and Joseph Fitzmyer recommends that the scriptural texts should not be made to say any more than they say. In Brown's judgment, "the totality of the scientifically controllable evidence leaves an unresolved problem."[21] The Lutheran-Roman Catholic scholars also recognize "the inability of a modern scientific approach to trace it to the stage of historicity."[22] Karl Rahner adds that questions involved in the doctrine of the virgin birth must be thought of afresh.[23] Leonardo Boff offers a further word of caution:

Intimately as it may belong to the permanent faith of the Church, the doctrine of Mary's perpetual virginity does not occupy a central place in the hierarchy of truths....Today, then, when the marian truths are no longer accepted without question, so that they must be continually defended and justified, the need arises for a distinction between what belongs to the *essential* content of faith, and what belongs to a secondary level.[24]

Influences of Docetism

The earliest heresy to plague Christianity was docetism.[25] According to the Docetists, matter is bad. Its proponents—and they were many—held that Jesus Christ only "appeared" to be human. His humanity was apparent, but not real. He was really God "dressed up" in human costume. He could not really be human, since earthly, fleshly humanity would be beneath the dignity of God. Though this thinking emerged (and was condemned) as early as the first century after Jesus' birth, it has reemerged and infected certain strains of Christian thought and piety ever since. From the early legends describing Jesus' birth, through medieval speculation on his superhuman knowledge, one gets the impression that, divine Son of God that he was, Jesus only "played the part" of being human, whether in Bethlehem, in Galilee, or on the cross. The seventeenth-century Jansenist tendency and its more recent expression in fundamentalist Christianity also tend to deny the human (with regard to Jesus and to ourselves). For many Christians of goodwill Jesus has become overspiritualized, abstract, and totally removed from our human condition.

The Docetists of the second century held that materiality, including human flesh, is evil. They believed that Jesus passed through Mary's body as through a tube or canal, thus denying his genuine full humanity and the normal processes by which he became a fully developed human being. The Council of Ephesus in 431 was very careful to insist that Jesus was born not only *through* Mary, (as if he had simply passed through her body), but *from* her, out of the very substance of her body. Jesus' first human contact was from, in, and with Mary his mother.

In his concern about such docetic tendencies, John McKenzie believes that the alleged evidence for the perpetual virginity of Mary does not withstand normal historical investigation. He therefore cautions:

It was easy to assume that the human vessel which served to bear the Incarnate Word should have been used exclusively for him and shared with no other, either before or after. It is less easy to assume that the vessel should have been preserved undamaged; for this implies a hidden supposition that parturition "damages" the feminine organs of reproduction. This in turn leads to a further suggestion that it is "better" that these organs never be used for their biological and social function.[26]

Karl Rahner is concerned to emphasize that God's grace achieved its most incomprehensible work where it laid hold of the world in the closest possible way in Mary. He says she "freely accepted the enfleshed Grace," which induced her "to allow the incarnation of the eternal God to happen in her, freely, through her faith, in order to share with the world this extreme nearness of God."[27]

Influences of Gnosticism

Gnosticism[28] was a movement present almost at the very beginning of Christianity. It survived into the fourth century, as is demonstrated in the Gnostic documents discovered in Nag Hammadi in Egypt in 1945.[29] The higher awareness that the Gnostics sought they called "*gnosis,*" meaning "knowledge" or "insight." They held that achieving this divine *gnosis* would redeem their spiritual being from the imprisonment of the flesh. In their yearning for truth and goodness they sought divine illumination through exploring the spiritual potential latent in the human psyche.[30] As a movement, Gnosticism preached a profound dualism between the material world of darkness and the spiritual world of light. Material existence, it taught, was radically evil, and human life was imprisoned in a creation controlled by sinister forces, space, and time.

Christian Gnostics wanted to go beyond elementary instruction in the faith and recover the sense of spiritual transformation they found in the message of Jesus. In the second century they heavily propagated the idea that Jesus did not come to die for humans, but came rather as an ambassador of God, bringing knowledge of God's being. Influenced by the views that identified sexuality with sin and sinfulness, they claimed that Jesus' birth did not pass the normal human processes. These Docetic and Gnostic views of the unreality of Jesus' humanity had to be countered to preserve the unity between Jesus' divinity and humanity.[31] The church did so by emphasizing Mary's virginity in Jesus' conception and birth. Mary's receptivity to the Holy Spirit became a key argument against these tendencies.[32]

Monastic and Ascetic Influences

During the third and fourth centuries the monastic and ascetic influences on the image of Mary put strong emphasis on her lifelong virginity. It was seen to be a model for lifelong virgins and celibates. The affirmation of Mary's virginity before, during, and after the birth of Jesus became even more emphasized. It was given exaggerated emphasis and became a model for virgins who adopted a "superior" way of life to that of married people. St. Ambrose of Milan declared Mary the special patroness of virgins.[33] When praising Mary's virginity he also depreciates sexuality and marriage.[34] For St. Jerome, too, virginity is superior to marriage. He also insists that Joseph was a virgin, "so that from a virgin wedlock, a virgin son was born."[35] St. Augustine, the most authoritative voice in Western Christian theology at that time, states: "A virgin conceived, a virgin gave birth, a virgin remained afterwards."[36] As a result devotion to Mary focused on her as virgin and mother, sometimes at the expense of woman and mother, as she is also portrayed in the gospels. The image presented by celibates and monks, however, did not penetrate deeply into the popular imagination, nor did it greatly influence the people's devotion to Mary. They continued to revere her as their personable and loving mother.

Raymond Brown is concerned about the fundamental difficulty of linking greater holiness to a life of virginity than to that of married life, and about using the scriptural texts about Mary's virginal conception of Jesus to support a life of vowed virginity. Unfortunately, he says, there has existed in Christian thought:

the attitude, explicit or implicit, that a virginal conception is a more noble way of conceiving a child than is marital intercourse; and this attitude is tied to the thesis that virginity is the nobler form of Christian life.[37]

Consequences of Such Interpretations

The patriarchal interpretation of the virginal motherhood of Mary has been inadequate, even disastrous, for the understanding of women's sexuality. First, it has encouraged the understanding that sexuality is principally procreative. Second, it has glorified the vocation of woman as that of mother in both biological and spiritual senses. Third, describing Mary's motherhood, as one hymn does, as "the one spotless womb wherein Jesus was laid," a mere receptacle of God's redeeming grace, is medieval and depersonalizing. Asking women to emulate the purity of the Virgin Mary and to serve unseen, as supposedly Mary did in the hidden Nazareth years, is a stumbling block to the achievement of self-affirmation for women. The principal difficulty for many lies in seeing Mary as virgin-mother, and in presenting this ideal as the model for women. As traditionally understood, this is an impossible ideal to follow.

Cultural Views of Virginity

Over the past decade, writers in both religion and psychology have shown an increased concern for the feminine in religion. Eric Neumann in his book *The Great Mother*[38] says that Mary's virginity symbolizes her creative independence rather than a rejection of her sexuality. The Virgin has stood for the caring, healing aspects conventionally associated with the feminine in people's psyche. If she were to disappear, patriarchal culture would dominate. Fortunately, it is impossible to erase a gentle presence that has existed for centuries in people's consciousness.

Theologians also are studying insights from cultural anthropologists about the culture of the Mediterranean world, where belief in the virginal conception emerged. In the Mediterranean world the great goddesses were often portrayed as virgins despite their consorts (Ishtar, Isis, Astarte). When used in relationship to these goddesses the term virginity did not necessarily connote bodily integrity or sexual abstinence, but female independence.[39]

Virginity symbolizes receptivity, a radical openness that actively reaches toward the transcendent God. The virginity of Mary, like the virginity of Israel, symbolizes her integrity of spirit and her absorption in God, as is evident in her surrender at the annunciation. In her cooperation with grace, she grew from grace to grace, and experienced herself as the unique creation of God.

In a world of exploitation and deprivation, the symbol of Mary's virginity can offer hope. Because of the degrading conditions of poverty in which many people live, especially in developing countries, countless persons are deprived of their identity, dignity, and personhood. The degradation is even more painful for Asian women who are forced to become part of the cheap labor market with inhuman and dangerous working conditions. They are often vulnerable to sexual exploitation, which sometimes leads to prostitution. In Mary's virginity, abused personhood is rehabilitated, crushed identity is restored, and those who are considered useless are called to be trusted messengers. We must appreciate the powerful symbol of the virginity of Mary and the intuitive wisdom of its cult, which has always existed alongside official pronouncements and theological debates, some of which have had little influence on the lives of the majority of Christians.

Questions for Reflection and Discussion

1. Dogmas speak to us and to our spirituality. How does a reflection on the *Theotokos*, Mary's Divine Motherhood, help to deepen and enrich our commitment to birth God in our world?

2. Because Christian spirituality was influenced by gnostic and dualistic thinking, it has led to some body-despising attitudes and practices. List and discuss these.

3. The doctrine of the virginal conception of Jesus points to his mysterious origins in God. Explain.

4. How might the dogma of Mary's virginity enrich our spirituality today? What hope does it offer us in a world where so many are deprived of their dignity and personhood?

Suggestions for Further Reading

Brown, Raymond E. *The Virginal Conception and the Bodily Resurrection of Jesus.* New York: Paulist Press, 1973, pp. 21-68.

Gebara Ivone, and Bingemer, Maria C. *Mary, Mother of God, Mother of the Poor.* Maryknoll, NY: Orbis Books, 1989, pp. 108-127.

Graef, Hilda. *Mary: A History of Doctrine and Devotion.* London: Sheed and Ward, 1963, Vol I, pp. 32-161.

Malina, Bruce, ed. *Biblical Theology Bulletin*, Vol 20 (Summer 1990), No 2. The entire issue is on Mary.

CHAPTER THREE

THE MARIAN DOGMAS II

In Chapter Two we sketched the historical development and theological implications of two ancient dogmas, Mary's divine motherhood and her virginity. This chapter traces the long evolution and development of two modern dogmas, the immaculate conception and the assumption. As eschatological symbols these dogmas offer a powerful impetus to living compassionately and justly. They also point to the final realization of the kingdom of God and offer us the hope of one day sharing fully in that kingdom when finally all are one in Christ (Galatians 3:28).

I. The Immaculate Conception

The doctrine of Mary's immaculate conception, unlike that of her motherhood and virginity, is not stated in the New Testament, nor can it be deduced from it. Nevertheless, it cannot be dismissed as mariolatry or superstition, for it is the fruit of a long historical evolution in popular Christian devotion, a devotion that has continued to assert itself against the opposition of theologians and bishops. The history of the evolution of the dogma of the immaculate conception is a 750-year history of stormy controversy between eminent theologians, religious communities of men, and curial congregations.

The term "immaculate conception" is alien to the thought patterns and worldview of first-century Judaism. A conception and birth for a Jewish family was a cause for rejoicing, a sign of divine favor. John the Baptist's conception and birth were regarded by Elizabeth and Zachariah as such a favor.

The very term "immaculate conception" can be misleading; it is therefore necessary to say what it is *not*. It is *not* a teaching about Mary's physical conception or about the process by which she came to life in her mother's womb. We must move away from the merely biological understanding of conception and consider the theological question behind the dogma, which states that Mary, from the first moment of her conception, was preserved from original sin.

In the important ecumenical study mentioned previously, *Mary in the New Testament*, the authors emphasize Mary's importance for the history of salvation. Her holiness, as emphasized in Luke 1 and 2 and in Matthew 1, seems to have been a strong influence in the development of the doctrine of the immaculate conception.[1]

The History of the Dogma of the Immaculate Conception

Once the doctrine of original sin was clarified in the Western tradition, it was natural that questions about Mary and original sin would arise. The doctrine of original sin became prominent because of the influence of St. Augustine (354-430). Augustine's debates, especially with Pelagius and his follower, the young Julian of Eclanum, an Italian bishop, engaged Christians from Rome to Africa. (The Eastern church, however, was almost completely free of the influence of Augustinian thought. Some Orthodox theologians are of the opinion that if the East had maintained the doctrine of original sin, it would probably have accepted the dogma of the immaculate conception when it was defined in 1854.) Augustine's understanding of original sin has greatly influenced the traditional understanding of the dogma of Mary's immaculate conception. We will first outline the evolution of the dogma that was officially defined in 1854.

Theological Arguments

The New Testament is silent about Mary's conception. Some early church fathers emphasized Mary's holiness, but did not consider her completely sinless. In the East, Origen, the great third-century theologian, did not believe Mary to be without fault.[2] In his view her faith wavered, like that of the apostles. A century later, John Chrysostom, the golden-mouthed patriarch of Constantinople, stressed her supposed faults and imperfections, which deserved to be reproved by her divine Son.[3] Athanasius (c. 296-373), the great defender of the divinity of Christ against its Arian opponents at the Council of Nicea (325), presented Mary as a model of holiness, but one whose good works were not perfect.[4]

In the West, Irenaeus, bishop of Lyons (d. 202), the first of the great theologians of Christendom, did not consider Mary free from all human fault.[5] Tertullian attributed less influence to Mary than did Irenaeus, and was ready to ascribe faults, if not sins, to her.[6] The image of the perfect, immaculate virgin had not yet emerged in the minds of the fourth-century fathers. Such doubts continued until the fifth century when the official proclamation of her divine motherhood at the Council of Ephesus in 431 accented her holiness.

Mary's purity and holiness had always been praised in glowing terms in the East. In the West, however, the language about Mary was far more restrained. Her queenship and power of intercession were treated much more soberly. Finally, in about the seventh century in the West, the question of her exemption from original sin was raised.

The gradual acceptance of her holiness, as expressed in the term "immaculate conception," was more the result of popular Christian piety and prayer than scholarly, theological reflection. There was a growing recognition of Mary's holiness and of our right to praise her beyond all other human beings and to say that she was as holy as any redeemed creature could be—"our tainted nature's solitary boast" as William Wordsworth described her. In the words of Herbert McCabe, Mary's immaculate conception "was a victory for the affective, over neat, rational systems, it was a liberation of the human spirit."[7] It was handed down not as a statement of fact but as a matter of prayer.

One of the critical stages in the development of the doctrine of the immaculate conception began with the writings of Eadmer (d. 1130), a disciple of St. Anselm. He argued that Mary's immaculate conception was possible: "God certainly could do it; if therefore he willed it, he did it." (*Potuit, decuit, fecit:* it was possible, it was fitting, therefore it was done).[8] The result of this maxim in mariology was often unfortunate, for what theologians deemed appropriate was often unwise and without foundation. Many possibilities—for example, that Mary should have had the beatific vision while on earth—were argued in this manner.

A thousand years after Mary's death, both Thomas Aquinas and

Bernard of Clairvaux explicitly denied the immaculate conception. Aquinas did not deny the sanctification of Mary before her birth; his difficulty lay to some extent in his theories about the beginnings of a human person and in particular with his view that animation is subsequent to conception.

A more important reason for the opposition was christological. The idea of an immaculate conception was seen as a threat to the unique and central place of Christ himself. Both Bernard and Aquinas raised the question: how holy could a redeemed creature be? They argued that one cannot be rescued unless one first has been captured. To say that Mary had never been captured, that is, that she had never been identified with the structures of injustice and sin, seemed to mean that she did not need redemption, that she did not need Christ. If Mary at her conception was free from original sin, then Christ's unique and saving redemption would thereby be rendered superfluous.

The dilemma was solved about the year 1300 by an Irish Franciscan, Duns Scotus (1264-1308). He developed the idea of preservative redemption as being a more perfect one: to have been preserved free from original sin was a greater grace than to be set free from sin. Scotus pointed out that not only is prevention better than cure, but that all cure aspires to being prevention.[9] He considered original sin a lack, a privation in our human nature, and he believed that this privation did not exist for Mary because a redemption that preserves from sin is more perfect than one that frees from sin. The very purpose of Christ's coming was to bring us the fullness of life. In Mary's case this redemption was anticipatory. The debate did not end with Scotus, but his position solved the principal christological objection.

For several centuries Dominican theologians followed St. Thomas in denying the doctrine of the immaculate conception, but by the nineteenth century they too had accepted it. By then it had continued to grow in popular devotion, art, and liturgy.

The Definition of the Dogma of the Immaculate Conception, 1854

The dogma of the immaculate conception was promulgated by Pius IX in the papal bull *Ineffabilis Deus* on December 8, 1854. It states that the Blessed Virgin Mary was free from original sin from the first moment of her existence:

> We declare...that the Most Blessed Virgin Mary in the first moment
> of her conception was, by the unique grace and privilege of God, in
> view of the merits of Jesus Christ the Savior of the human race, pre-
> served intact from all stain of original sin.[10]

The dogma was promulgated to the resistance of some Catholics and
the shock of Protestants. Objections came from Orthodox, Anglican, and
Protestant theologians. The Anglicans objected not because they rejected
the proclamation's essential teaching but because they thought it should
not have been proposed as a dogma.[11]

The language of the proclamation is that of mid-nineteenth-century
Catholic dogmatic theology. In its expression it tends to have a negative
tone. The language is impersonal and too far removed from the ordinary
life experience of most Christians to be appreciated for its meaning. Yet
we must pay attention not so much to the actual formulation as to the
essential meaning that the words seek to convey, but which we today
might express differently.

The proclamation states that Mary is preserved intact from all stain of
original sin. Mary's holiness is discussed in terms of original sin, and sin
is understood as stain. For us today, this is too negative and passive a way
of expressing what is intended. Because the doctrine of original sin has
influenced our understanding of Mary as having been conceived without
sin, we need to examine the teaching of original sin that has been taught
to Christians through the centuries.

The Classical Doctrine of Original Sin

Except for a few minor points, the church's official doctrine of original
sin has come down to us from St. Augustine. Augustine taught that when
Adam and Eve misused their gift of freedom and refused to accept their
creaturely status, evil emerged in the world. From then on, humanity was
no longer oriented to the good. Desire, a natural tendency, becomes, after
the "fall," an enslaving concupiscence. Through the sin of Adam and Eve
an original condition characterized by moral and physical integrity has
been lost. This sin influences every descendent of the human race at the
moment of his or her coming into being, a hereditary taint, as it were,
passed along in the genes. Only the grace of God in Jesus Christ can bring
salvation. Traditional sermons on original sin have often emphasized this

catastrophe befallen an innocent creation through the sin of our early ancestors at the dawn of history. Also, the anachronistic tendency to read Augustine's position back into the narrative of our first parents in Genesis 3, and the reading of that myth as history, has reinforced pessimistic views of sexuality and human nature in western Christianity and colored western culture ever since.

Augustine's theological formulation derived from his reflection on the torturous experience of his own conversion, his interpretation of the Scriptures, especially Genesis 2 and 3 and Romans 5, and finally his controversies with Gnosticism and Pelagianism. The Manichaean Gnostics believed that human life was imprisoned in a creation controlled by sinister forces, and yet it possessed a yearning for truth and goodness outside of space and time. Evil was a contagion infecting the person from without. The only hope was to escape from this material universe to the realm of the divine. Pelagianism, on the other hand, asserted human freedom against Manichaean fatalism and emphasized the God-given human capacity to do good. The desire for, and the realization of, the good lies within human nature. Because all people are fundamentally free to choose good or evil, one could theoretically live without sin, though such a case would be exceedingly rare.

Augustine developed his theology of original sin as a response both to the pessimistic dualism of the Gnostics and to Pelagius' simplistic reduction of sin to a conscious free choice of evil. We cannot overestimate the impact of his theology on centuries of Christian piety and thought. "His views prevailed, eclipsing for future generations of western Christians the consensus of more than three centuries of Christian tradition."[12] The Augustinian teaching was supported by later councils and more especially by the Council of Trent, which solemnly defined that Adam, by his disobedience, lost the original holiness and justice and incurred through his sin the wrath of God and death. Trent also extended to the descendants of Adam the consequences of Adam's sin.

Because the immaculate conception was historically understood in terms of original sin, the above overview of Augustine's theology should help us grasp the literal interpretation often given to the dogma of Mary's immaculate conception. The wording of the definition—being preserved intact from all stain of original sin—suggests that Mary was spared the catastrophe that had befallen human nature at the beginning of history.

Contemporary Reflections on Original Sin

Theology today is drawing upon contemporary psychological and anthropological insights to describe the universal human condition traditionally known as original sin. Reflections on the human condition help us to gain a deeper understanding into the history of sin and how it is passed on. Instead of interpreting it as a penalty inherited for the crime of a primal ancestor, it needs to be understood in the context of the conflictual experiences and growth of any maturing personality. We come into a world that has already been shaped by the sinful decisions of others and by sinful situations—the responsibility of which cannot really be laid on anyone individually, but can be laid on everyone collectively. The evil or hurt done to one generation often affects the next. Our worldviews and biases, and those of our culture, are passed on to the next generation, which unconsciously internalizes them. Sin has incarnated itself in values, in customs, in prejudices and biases, in wrong convictions, and in unjust institutions and structures of society. It is this cycle of evil, "this chain reaction," into which we enter when we come into this world, to which the doctrine of the "inheritance" of original sin points.

Gil Bailie in his book *Violence Unveiled*[13] suggests that we examine Rene Gerard's groundbreaking study of the central role of *mimesis* in human experience. *Mimesis* is the human preference for imitation. We are imitative creatures; we "ape," or mimic, others. But *mimesis* is more powerful and less consciously intentional than the merely conscious act of imitation. We desire what someone else desires. This is what generates conflict and leads to rivalry and violence. Violence in turn invites more violence. Bailie believes that a study of *mimesis* and the mimetic mechanism that produces violence and gives it its mystifying power may be the most important contribution to our understanding of original or universal sinfulness since Augustine.[14]

Contemporary theology,[15] emphasizing the universality of grace, counters the anthropological pessimism of Augustine and focuses on our universal hunger for healing and wholeness, integrity and transformation. We *can* break the cycle of evil by refusing to be carriers of evil. We *can* face the fears and frustrations that prevent us from believing that we are desirable persons who can and must be healed. In supportive relationships, in prayer, or in therapy we confront our compulsive behaviors and allow into consciousness the hurts and wrongs done to us in the past. We learn from Jesus to forgive our enemies and accept the hurts of life without passing them on. By God's grace we *can* grow into affectionate, imaginative persons, caring and sharing, and living in profound interior communion with one another. Finally, the doctrine of original sin focuses on our need for redemption and points to the future kingdom where "death shall be no more, neither shall there be mourning nor crying nor pain" (Revelation 21:4).

Interpreting the Doctrine of the Immaculate Conception

In declaring Mary's original sinlessness, the dogma celebrates God's victory over the powers and principalities of this world in the coming into existence of this woman, Mary. In her very being, through the gracious mercy of God, the grip of evil is broken. While not removing her from the sufferings of this world, grace was freely given to her from the first moment of her existence because she was destined to be the mother of Jesus. This grace enabled her to live in constant union with God from the beginning. Her response in faith to God brought Christ into the world, and through Christ sin loses its power over the world.

In affirming Mary's immaculate conception, we profess that in a woman, Mary, the Mother of God, ultimate meaning for the whole of reality, material and spiritual, is already realized. We profess that this hopeless state of frustration and alienation, of being enmeshed in the sinful structures of society, has come to an end in her. In Mary we see what it means to be redeemed. The symbol of original sin points to an unfaithful world. The symbol of the immaculate conception shows that even the accumulated sinfulness of the world cannot overcome God's desire to save. It is therefore an eschatological symbol, a strong foundation for Christian hope, and a powerful impetus to a Christian commitment to justice in a world of global violence and exploitation.

On the personal level, our lives are crisscrossed with pain and anxiety and sometimes too with a sense of worthlessness and meaninglessness, especially when we encounter death. The symbol of the immaculate conception reminds us that all of life is ultimately good and meaningful. It will find its fulfillment in the final coming of the kingdom.

Our language, worldview, values, life-styles, and preferences are already molded and shaped by the socioeconomic and political systems that control our lives. Society often makes the fruits of production available only to the rich. Laws tend to make for stability and to freeze society in favor of the rich and powerful; and culture supports such unjust economic and political structures. Religion, too, is often used to legitimate and support these unjust structures.

A greater leap of the imagination is needed to grasp the nuclear issue. Jonathan Schell[16] remarks that there are approximately twenty thousand megatons of nuclear explosives now in existence, and that one megaton alone equals the explosive yield of eighty Hiroshimas. The immaculate conception is a symbol that summons us to political and ecological action and reminds us that we may not take a neutral position. It is an eschatological symbol that points to where we are going and offers us the hope that we shall arrive.

The Immaculate Conception: Its Significance as Archetype

An archetype is "the essential core of a pattern of universal symbols" that come to us from our collective unconscious and deal with archaic or "primordial types, that is, with universal images that have existed since the remotest times."[17] The symbol of the immaculate conception points to a purity of reality and consciousness, prior to "knowing good and evil," a reality, prior to and without sin or suffering, present in all of us at the core of our being. It is at this core that we experience God's divine and graceful presence within us. This is our truest self, our being at one with everything. It is a reality that we possessed "in the beginning," and that cannot cease to exist. We have only lost sight of it, for our original unity remains. That there should be at least one point in us that is free is a great discovery. The mystery of the immaculate conception is about us, for in Mary we discover our true self.[18] This is the significance of the immaculate conception as archetype.

However, it is not this true self that we ordinarily experience. The myth of the "fall" suggests the puzzling and unexplainable fact that we are alienated from that true self. To awaken to the presence of our true self, the false self, which keeps us on the surface of reality, must die. This awakening is actually a recovery, since the true self is always there. In this awakening we discover our oneness with God, and in God with all of reality. Being attentive to this oneness is what Thomas Merton calls contemplation:

by being attentive, by learning to listen (or recovering the natural capacity to listen which cannot be learned any more than breathing), we can find ourselves engulfed in such happiness that it cannot be explained; the happiness of being at one with everything in the hidden ground of Love for which there can be no explanation.[19]

It is of the very necessity of our being that we *be* in God. This contemplative dimension of our being is present even if we never advert to it. Contemplative prayer brings to the surface of our lives this fundamental awareness by which we become aware of ourselves and of all things in God. Very often people arrive at this full awakening of the true self only in death. Because we are often so overly rational, driven to achieve and control, we may not be attentive to the divine presence within us. Mary, who never lost sight of the divine presence within her, is our model of contemplation. She also knew that God's grace is superior to the reigning power of evil, and that because of the goodness of God's superabundant love the world is never without God's presence and compassion. Mary experienced what it is like to grow in grace and contemplation, living in ecstatic enjoyment of her God and of God's creation.

In Mary we see the destiny of the church. Like Virgin Israel, she is set apart from the world, reserved for Yahweh. The virginity of Mary and her immaculate conception are at one here. In Mary conceived without sin, we see what we are to be. She reminds us that saintliness is possible. In the radically holy Virgin Mary, we see the destiny of the church that is to be "without spot or wrinkle, or any such thing, that she might be holy and immaculate" (Ephesians 5:27), until finally "all are one in Christ" (Galatians 3:28).

II. Mary's Assumption

Scripture gives us no specific information about Mary's assumption. From the earliest centuries, however, Christians seemed to have been convinced about Mary's extraordinary holiness and her place in God's plan. They believed that she who was exceptional all through her life, by God's design, must have an exceptional final destiny too. And so they were gradually led to affirm her bodily assumption. The earliest discussion of Mary's death is in the writings of Epiphanius (d. 403). He gives two possibilities—that she died or did not—and he then confesses that he does not know which is true.

It took six centuries before writings on the assumption were recorded, possibly because of the bizarre and legendary details in apocryphal writings about Mary during that time. Then we find the first homilies on the assumption from Theotoknos of Livia. (His homilies were published only in 1955 and so were unavailable to Pope Pius XII who proclaimed the assumption a dogma in 1950.)

Theotoknos followed the Greek tradition of grace, which is seen as divinizing, so he stressed the connection between virginity, grace, and incorruption. From as early as the fifth century there was a strong conviction that Mary's body did not corrupt in the tomb, but was taken up shortly after death, reunited with its soul, and transformed by the power of the Spirit. In the sixth century, belief in her assumption was associated with the celebration of her feast day, which, like that of all the other saints, was observed on the day of her death. An apocryphal narrative claiming to give details about her death, funeral, empty tomb, and bodily reception into heaven coalesced with the celebration of her feast.[20] Then in various Eastern churches the feast of the Falling Asleep of the Mother of God, the *Theotokos*, the Ever-Virgin, the All Holy One, became a popular liturgical celebration. It spread to Rome about the middle of the seventh century, where it became her main feast day.

Belief in this doctrine developed mainly through preaching and devotional literature. In view of Mary's mission as Mother of God, it was fitting that she taste death but not that she undergo the corruption of the tomb. Though the doctrine of the assumption was believed in the East and its feast celebrated, doubts were expressed in the West in works ascribed to Jerome and Augustine, as well as St. Bede (d. 735), and St. Adhanan of Iona (d. 1040).

The Proclamation of the Dogma

The bodily assumption of the Blessed Virgin Mary was defined as a dogma of faith by Pius XII in 1950. The definition states:

By the authority of Our Lord Jesus Christ, of the blessed Apostles, Peter and Paul, and by our own, we proclaim and define it to be a dogma revealed by God, that the immaculate Mother of God, Mary ever Virgin, when the course of her earthly life was finished, was taken up body and soul into the glory of heaven.[21]

This proclamation says nothing about Mary's death or about how she died, but cautiously talks about "when the course of her earthly life was finished." Pius XII speaks of her assumption (*analepsis*), not dormition (*koimesis*):

> It was fitting that the most holy body of Mary, the God bearing body, the receptacle of God, which was divinized, incorruptible, illumined by divine grace and full of glory…should be entrusted to the earth for a short while and be raised up in glory to heaven, with her soul pleading to God.[22]

Her life on earth is over and her commitment to, and association with, Jesus, which began at the incarnation, has now entered a final, perfect stage. To proclaim Mary's assumption as a dogma of faith is to affirm that she now shares in the fullness of the resurrection that God promised all peoples when God raised Jesus from the dead. Thus Mary's assumption depends totally on Christ's resurrection. She now lives beyond death, beyond judgment, and the same glory that she now enjoys is what we, by God's mercy, hope to enjoy eventually.

Alluding to the bloody wars of the twentieth century and to the growth of materialism, the papal decree deplores how the destruction of life and the desecration of the human body threaten the sense of our God-given identity. By holding forth Mary as our model, "the exalted destiny of both our soul and body may in this striking manner be brought clearly to the notice of all persons."[23]

The Second Vatican Council emphasized the unity of Mary's bodily and spiritual glory in heaven. The assumption "body and soul" asserts that the whole person will be saved. Christian faith teaches that, at the resurrection of the dead, every person receives a transformed body (not the corpse that is left behind) and is taken entirely into eternal life, since the soul cannot be separated from the body. Though Mary was sinless, she was not exempt from the final transformation in death. In our desperate search for immortality we often see death as an obstacle to be overcome. Death is not punishment; it belongs properly to the human life God wills for humankind. The relationship between the church and the Virgin assumed into heaven is stressed in *Lumen Gentium*:

In the meantime the Mother of Jesus in the glory which she possesses in body and soul in heaven is the image and the beginning of the Church as it is to be perfected in the world to come. Likewise she shines forth on earth, until the day of the Lord shall come, a sign of certain hope and comfort to the pilgrim People of God.[24]

The Second Vatican Council urges us to pray that Mary intercede with Christ as she did at the beginnings of the church, "until all the peoples of the human family are happily gathered into the one People of God for the glory of the Most Holy Trinity."[25] In her assumption, Mary is a sign of the future fulfillment of the church and a comfort to us pilgrim people.

When the assumption was declared a dogma of faith in 1950, many people feared that it might be another major block to Christian unity. Ironically, it was the Protestant psychiatrist Carl Jung who saw this as the most important religious event in four hundred years. Jung felt that a materialistic worldview, combined with the progress of science and technology, endangered the spiritual heritage of humankind. The church, he said, needed a feminine symbol. He realized that the newly aware consciousness of the dignity of women must be consciously recognized and given symbolic statement. He even called Mary the "fourth person" of the Trinity. Jung is not making a theological statement here, nor is he incorporating Mary into the Godhead. He is concerned with the fact that by raising the feminine (often projected as a symbol of evil) to the level of the divine, the church was making a powerful symbolic statement. To see the woman Mary crowned and glorious in heaven was to see the feminine in a new light.

In the body of Mary glorified, material creation begins to participate in the risen body of Christ.[26] Mary's assumption not only anticipates the resurrected body of all Christians but the redeemed state of the cosmos, which at present is subject to decay:

The material world's completed redeemed state must also shine forth in Mary as Archetype of the church...the redeemed state of the physical cosmos at the end of time shines forth in her body.[27]

In a century that has experienced terrible wars, massive destruction of human life and of centers of civilization, the exploitation of our ecology, and the constant threat of nuclear war, the Catholic church has affirmed that, in a woman, Mary, the Mother of God, ultimate meaning for the whole of reality is already realized. We feel helpless in the midst of the poverty, famine, and oppression that bring untimely death to millions of women, men, and children. We are encouraged, however, by such developments as networking for solidarity and caring for our planet Earth. These are signs of hope amid injustice and oppression. The immaculate conception and the assumption point to the final fulfillment of the kingdom of God and challenge us to work for the transformation of the present as we look forward to the fullness of time, gathering up "all things in him, things in heaven and things on earth" (Ephesians 1:10).

Questions for Reflection and Discussion

1. Traditional theology viewed original sin as a penalty inherited for the crime of our primal ancestors. How do contemporary insights help us to discuss the dogma of original sin without falling into anthropological pessimism?

2. The mystery of Mary's immaculate conception points to the experience of God's graceful presence within us. What message does this dogma have for the living out of our call to contemplation and mysticism?

3. The immaculate conception is an eschatological symbol and a powerful impetus to commit ourselves to living justly and compassionately. Discuss.

4. Discuss the cosmic significance of the dogma of Mary's assumption in the context of the contemporary ecological exploitation of our world.

Suggestions for Further Reading

Coyle, Kathleen. "Original Sin: Residue of Some Primal Crime?" *East Asian Pastoral Review*, Vol 29, No 3, 1992.

Gebara, Ivone and Bingemer, Maria C. *Mary Mother of God, Mother of the Poor.* Maryknoll, NY: Orbis Books, 1989, pp. 108-127.

Flanagan, Donal. *The Theology of Mary.* Hales Corners, WI: Clergy Book Service, 1976.

Primavesi, Anne. *From Apocalypse to Genesis: Ecology Feminism and Christianity.* Minneapolis: Fortress Press, 1991, pp. 222-264.

CHAPTER FOUR

EVERY AGE FORMS ITS OWN IMAGE OF MARY

While theologians addressed questions of doctrine in the evolution and development of theological thought about Mary, the ordinary faithful continued to show an intense reverence toward the Mother of God in prayer and devotion. We will concern ourselves here with the pious practices of generations of Christians as they largely shaped their own image of Mary, and as she adapted herself to their religious needs in various times and places.

From early days, devotion to Mary found expression within the liturgy. A prayer of petition to her *Sub Tuum Praesidium* ("Under your protection, O Holy Mother of God...") is attested from the late third or fourth century.[1] This prayer, which was adopted into the Byzantine, Coptic, Ethiopian, and Latin churches, shows us the early development of belief in Mary's intercession being expressed in prayer. There was a strong mutual influence between prayer and belief, and the development of popular piety reflected the people's traditional belief in her powerful intercession. Since the fourth century, marian hymns have been sung, and churches have been named after her.

Marian Devotion after Ephesus

It is probably safe to say that the real impetus for the marian cult began at the Council of Ephesus in 431, when Mary's unique role as *Theotokos*, the Godbearer, was defined (as we have seen in Chapter Two). Although

the focus of this decision was christological, it gave a great impetus to
marian devotion. After Ephesus feasts multiplied and devotions became
more fervent. Mary's purity, which had been praised in such glowing
terms, led to questions about the decomposition of her body in death. In
fact, death seemed no longer compatible with the dignity of the Mother
of God. She was the awe-inspiring *Theotokos* in whom the very transcendence of the Creator was reflected. Poets and hymn writers used a variety
of Old Testament typology to describe her:

> Mountain of God; bush unconsumed by fire; Aaron's rod which
> blossomed; ark of imperishable wood; lampstand of pure gold
> which bears the lamp which burns forever; jar of gold which con-
> cealed the manna; Jacob's ladder by which Jesus came down to
> earth; the queen which stands at the king's right hand.[2]

The central idea of Eastern spirituality is the theology of deification by
grace. Mary is the human being who most resembles the perfect image of
God, the incarnate Word. In her the divine image can be contemplated.
Because God's incarnation as the Christ was at the center of the Eastern
church's theology, Mary was praised as the great *Theotokos*. She has
reached the final glorification toward which the church aspires. She is the
one *par excellence* who has contemplated God. Pope John Paul II's encyclical letter *Redemptoris Mater* says of the churches in the East:

> The Greek Fathers and the Byzantine tradition, contemplating the
> Virgin in the light of the Word made flesh, have sought to penetrate
> the depth of the bond which unites Mary, as Mother of God to
> Christ and the Church....Such a wealth of praise, built up by the
> different forms of the Church's great tradition, could help us to has-
> ten the day when the Church can begin once more to breathe fully
> with her "two lungs," the East and the West.[3]

The Desert Fathers and Mothers

In the Constantinian period, when the Christian religion was officially
tolerated and was subsequently adopted as the official state religion, the
threat of martyrdom had passed and the ideal of carrying one's cross
found expression in asceticism. Mary, Queen of Virgins, became the

patroness of ascetics and celibates. She was the model of women withdrawing to the Egyptian desert to lead a hermetic life.[4] Documents from this period describe her as a perfect Egyptian nun, eating and sleeping only when her body demanded it. She avoided her relatives and other women who spoke of the things of this world, and made progress every day. She was perceived as a solitary, consorting only with angels and leading the life of the most exemplary austerity.

The Patristic Period

From the beginning of the third century there was continued interest in drawing a parallel between Eve and Mary to emphasize Mary's personal virtues. Whereas Eve's response to the divine command was disobedience, resulting in death, Mary obeyed God, thus becoming the mother of the savior. Through her obedience to God's will she reversed the disobedience of Eve, becoming the Virgin Mother of God. This theme is introduced by Justin Martyr[5] (d. circa 165) and becomes a favorite topic in patristic teaching. (We will deal at length with the Eve–Mary parallelism in Chapter Six.)

During the fourth century there was an upsurge in popular devotion to Mary. She became the ideal of the consecrated virgin who always stayed at home and prayed. (By contrast, the Mary of the gospels did not hesitate to visit her cousin Elizabeth and attend the Temple feasts).

In the fifth century the church fathers spoke of Mary as taking a vow of virginity. St. Augustine was the first of the Latin fathers to take a vow of virginity. Gradually the practice of taking a formal vow became an established custom in the church. It then seemed only fitting that Mary, the prototype of virgins, would have been the first to make such a promise to God. The imitation of Mary became an established way of life.

It may be a surprise to some to discover that as late as the time of Augustine there is no mention of hymns, prayers, or marian feasts in the West. Only in the fifth century do we have the first hymn directly saluting Mary. Her name was not inserted into the Roman Canon until the sixth century. The titles "Mother of Mercy" and "Mater Dolorosa" were applied to her in the sixth century. The feasts of her annunciation, "dormition," and purification were not adopted in the West until the seventh century.

By the end of the patristic period properly so called, the main doctrinal and devotional lines had been traced. Mariology as well as marian liturgy and marian poetry had reached a far more advanced stage in the East than in the West. In the West, as we have noted, the language about Mary was far more restrained. The context for devotion and praise was both doctrinal and liturgical. Under the influence of Tertullian and Augustine, and with theology's preoccupation with original sin, Mary's grace-filled figure was contemplated as a type of the church itself. Her intimate relationship with the church was affirmed by St. Ambrose and St. Augustine. St. Ambrose, who may be called the father of western mariology,[6] asks us to imitate Mary who was "a virgin and humble of heart" and "as Mary did, do also in your heart." The question of whether Mary was exempt from original sin appears not even to have been asked at this stage. Her assumption seems to have been accepted only in Gaul, her queenship and power of intercession are treated much more soberly, and there is no question yet of her mediation.

The Early Middle Ages

In the later Byzantine period the first author to have attempted a life of Mary was Epiphanius the Monk (d. circa 800). He used a lot of apocryphal material as well as New Testament data and presented her according to the Byzantine ideal of beauty. He described her grave and dignified bearing "with light brown hair and eyes, black eyebrows, a straight nose, a long face and long hands and fingers."[7]

In the eighth century in the West we find the influence of the Greeks on Latin mariology, due to the many Greek monks who had settled in Sicily to escape the persecution of the emperors. They blended the splendor of the Byzantine image of the glorious queen, mistress of heaven and earth, interceding on our behalf, with that of the tender mother giving her maternal love and tenderness to all.

The first aspect of medieval marian devotion arose from sheer delight in what God had done for her, and what she in turn had done to realize God's designs in the world. Central to this devotion was the graciousness of Mary's *fiat* at the annunciation. During the Middle Ages, the handmaid of the Lord, as she is described in Luke's Magnificat, became "Our Lady," an acting subject with an important relationship to the person seeking salvation. There was also a shift from a liturgical perspective to a personal one, and this was expressed in the proliferation of new devotions.

The Middle Ages

As European culture revived, the cult of Mary began to grow. Crowds flocked to attend the monastery festivals connected with the marian feasts. Together with the monks, the faithful contemplated the beauty and the glory of the Virgin Mary. A flourishing trade led to the rebirth of towns and the rise of a new merchant class. Glorious Gothic cathedrals were built, usually dedicated to Mary, and sophisticated schools of theology sprang up. By the twelfth century devotion to Mary was widespread. In fact this century is known as the golden age of mariology.

Theological reflection on Mary was chiefly developed by the Cistercians, especially St. Bernard of Clairvaux. Bernard fostered a form of meditative writing that expressed an intense devotion to her. This affective approach continued for a long time to come. It was the age of the Crusades, of feudalism, and of courtly love. These developments also had their influence on marian doctrine and devotion. Mary was hailed in chivalrous terms as the fair lady of the knights—"Our Lady" and "Madonna"—respectful titles given to feudal aristocrats. They were both symbols of chaste love. Mary, a simple Palestinian housewife, could not meet the needs of the aristocratic ladies. Before they could venerate her they had to make her one of themselves. From the simple maiden of Nazareth she became the great Queen of Heaven, assigned a place above the church, between God and the highest angels.

Consciousness of sin and fear of judgment were characteristics of this era. The awesome figure of God the Father, as stern king and just judge, was difficult to approach. A high christology, too, tended to distance Christ from ordinary people. Like the distant feudal kings, he was too threatening to be approached directly. Such emphasis on the transcendent justice of God made it impossible for God to forgive sin without demanding satisfaction. Sinful people experienced the temptations of Satan and the dangers of eternal torment in hell as very real.

Divine mercy, however, found its expression in the mother of Jesus, who, like a kindhearted feudal noblewoman, could bend her son's ear and plead the cause of those who sought her intercession. Consequently, the enormous veneration poured out toward Mary expressed itself in the multiplication of prayers, relics, shrines, feasts, and narrations of miraculous cures. In the process, Mary often outshone Jesus and occasionally even God the Father. She was substituted for God as the acting subject of divine deeds and the recipient of divine glory and praise, as we note in a medieval version of the standard prayer, the *Te Deum*:

> We praise thee, O Mother of God; we confess thee, Mary ever Virgin....Thee all angels and archangels, thrones and principalities serve. Thee all powers and virtues in heaven and all dominations obey. Before thee all the angelic choirs, the cherubim and seraphim, exulting, stand. With unceasing voice every angelic creature proclaims thee: Holy, holy, holy, Mary, Virgin Mother of God.

Among the Latin preachers and theologians the doctrine of the immaculate conception became the topic of discussion and theological debate. They pondered over such questions as whether Mary had to struggle against sin, or whether she was conceived and sanctified by the Spirit from her mother's womb. The Augustinian doctrine of original sin played a decisive part in this controversy. St. Bernard, as we have seen in the previous chapter, opposed it on the grounds that it had no tradition behind it. On the other hand, popular religious literature embellished the biblical and apocryphal stories about Christ and his mother. Feasts in her honor became more and more elaborate; some were preceded by a vigil, others even by a two-week fast. In the sixteenth century, however, this exaggerated cult of the Virgin was stamped out by the reformers in all Protestant countries.

The intensification of interest in Mary in the medieval period, as well as the emphasis on her exalted role in human salvation, provided a "feminizing" element in an otherwise wholly male-dominated religion. It has been suggested that she replaced the mother goddess Christianity lacked; at the level of popular devotion, she occupied the place left vacant by Isis, Cybele, and the other goddesses.[8] However, her theological isolation from all other women prevented her from functioning psychologically as a model for female personhood.[9] Both in theology and in popular religiosity she assumed a personality that often reflected the male's idealized image of the female.

The Thirteenth Century

The ferment of intellectual life associated with the new universities began to change the social structures of monastic-centered Christianity. A new generation of people emerged, anxious to live the gospel outside the traditional monastic structure. The ministry of preaching to the laity was undertaken by the new mendicant orders, the Franciscans and Dominicans. They focused on Jesus in the poverty of his humanity; in scenes of the crib and the cross, Mary was always present in a human role. At the same time scholastic theology was developing an understanding of redemption that emphasized the need to make satisfaction for sin. The awe-inspiring Virgin Mother of Christ now became the Mother of Mercy, who mediates between Christ and sinners.

While the development of theological thought was then taking place outside the monasteries, the rigor of scholastic theology, with its emphasis on the faculty of reason, had little room for affectivity or imagination. Compounding the problem was that the language of scholarly discourse and liturgy was Latin. Latin liturgy and scholastic theology became ever more remote from the ordinary experience of people at a time when life was hard and often dangerous. Besides, scholastic theologians allotted little space to Mary. The immaculate conception continued to evoke theological discussion. As we saw in the last chapter, Duns Scotus initiated a new way of looking at this mystery. He asserted that Mary was equally dependent on Christ, whether Christ's grace preserved her from sin or sanctified her in the womb—the more common opinion at that time. Beyond this controversy, Mary appeared only in the great summas, and then only in relation to questions about the incarnation.

The people loved the Virgin, so it is natural to expect that other strains of marian piety and ways of venerating Mary would continue to come from the popular religious imagination of the people. The meditative writing initiated earlier by St. Bernard provided an opportunity to express an intense devotion to her, and it appealed to a wider and more popular audience.

The Fourteenth and Fifteenth Centuries

The earlier spirituality that focused on Mary's person now shifted from contemplation to a popular imagination that was less critical. In the imagination of the people there was intense reverence toward her. With her maternal influence over God she mediated God's grace to unworthy sinners. She functioned as a merciful and tender mother caring for her spiritual children. There were, however, lots of abuses prevalent in the mariology of this late medieval period. Focus on the mystery of the incarnation was now replaced by a magical idea of Mary as mother who could solve all problems. René Laurentin comments on the fourteenth century:

> Repelled by desiccated intellectualism, people sought life on the imaginative and sentimental plane. Throughout this period of decadence popular enthusiasm for the Blessed Virgin never faltered, but the adulterated fodder it was nourished on, consisted of trumpery miracles, ambiguous slogans, and inconsistent maundering.[10]

Because of such natural disasters as the Black Death, the experiences of the Hundred Years War, and the Great Western Schism, people prayed to Mary, Mother of Mercy, for her protection from dangers pressing from every side. When one-fifth of the population of Europe was wiped out by the Black Death, people sought consolation in the image of the sorrowing mother at the foot of the cross. The Franciscans encouraged the faithful to follow the Via Dolorosa, to journey with Mary to the cross. For Christians who could not afford to make the pilgrimage to Jerusalem, this was a way of sharing in the sufferings of Mary and her Son.

At times Mary's ability to rescue the sinner became the focus of devotion, so that she often functioned independent of God. Popular preaching designated her Queen of Heaven and Refuge of Sinners and placed her at the center of the process of personal salvation. Some have even understood such titles as Queen of Heaven to be the reemergence of the suppressed mother goddess of prehistoric times. While theologians today may interpret her usurpation of the role of Christ as a deterioration of mariology, anthropologists, on the other hand, analyze it as an appreciation of what has traditionally been termed the feminine element in the world. This feminine figure, which embodies the attributes of tenderness and compassion, grieves with the sorrowful rather than punishing them for their offenses. Devotion to the compassionate Mother of Mercy expressed a need for a religious experience of the feminine in the divine, an experience not available through the understanding of God at the time.

Because of a still underdeveloped theology of the Holy Spirit, the figure of Mary assumed the caring qualities of the divine. Catholic piety tended to view her as spiritually present to guide and inspire, to console and intercede, actions that in the Scriptures belong to the Spirit (John

14:16; 15:26). It was difficult, therefore, to focus on her as a creature of God and our model disciple. (We will pursue this discussion in Chapter Seven.)

While marian doctrine and devotion developed considerably between the eleventh and fifteenth centuries in the West, they remained more static in the East. This was because the influences of both the Augustinian doctrine of original sin as well as that of scholastic theology were absent there. In the West, too, the doctrine of original sin played a decisive part in the controversy about the immaculate conception.

The Sixteenth Century

The first challenge to the abuses and distortions of the late medieval church as well as to the popular cult of Mary came with the Reformation. Neither the immaculate conception nor the assumption had as yet been declared dogma. The Protestant reformers deplored the lack of trust in God's grace and mercy communicated through Christ alone. Protestant and Catholic thinkers alike objected to the excesses of popular belief. In his study on the early Reformation period, Carlos Eire shows that, in this period, religion sought to grasp the transcendent and make it immanent.[11] It sought to embody itself in images, to reduce the infinite to the finite and disintegrate all mystery. The magical and healing powers of relics, for example, led to their becoming objects of devotion. The wood of the cross was believed to have special powers to combat the devil.[12]

Martin Luther believed that human beings remain sinners, no matter what they do, God only imputing to them the merits of Christ. However, he could still admit that Mary could pray for us, as we pray for each other. Luther himself showed a tender devotion to the Virgin, especially in his early sermons. In his commentary on the Magnificat he described Mary as a woman of faith and our model of God's grace to the world. He retained a remarkable amount of Catholic teaching that was only dismissed by his successors. However, he equated the exaggerations of Catholic devotion to Mary with the cult of Baal, which was denounced by the prophets.[13] He stressed that the true basis of Mary's dignity was as a believer, and that any special blessings given to her were through the merits of Christ and not due to her own special merits.

The reformers did not turn against Mary in herself. They rejected her veneration on christological grounds. Luther's polemic was aimed essentially at what seemed to him to be the false honor done to Mary. He felt that "Christ was dispossessed and his "office" taken from him."[14] The reformers felt that praying to Mary and asking for favors detracted from Christ as the sole mediator between God and human beings. The response of the Council of Trent (1545-63) was cautious. It simply taught that it was good to invoke the saints, and it requested each local bishop to correct abuses.

Some contemporary Protestant writers are prepared to contend that Protestantism has made a serious mistake in its opposition to the Virgin:

> Ignoring the place of the Blessed Virgin in the Incarnation and the whole process of salvation has given Protestantism a harsh thoroughly masculine emphasis....The absence of tenderness and affection in Protestantism has led to an overemphasis on a harsh prophetic picture of God with its attending preoccupation with judgment....The development of a mature Mariology in Protestant thinking could do much to temper the harsh portrayal of the God of judgment and provide it with a healthy concept of a God of mercy.[15]

If anything, Protestant criticisms of the marian cult increased Catholic enthusiasm for it. Catholics multiplied their efforts to preserve her exalted status. This exalted image stands in stark contrast to that of the Virgin of Guadalupe who took the form of a simple Indian peasant woman when she appeared to Juan Diego in Mexico in 1531 and affirmed the indigenous people over against the Spanish conquerors. (The significance of this apparition is discussed at length in the Appendix.)

The Seventeenth Century

In the seventeenth century, a hundred years after the Reformation, marian devotions reached a second peak, especially in France, which emerged as the spiritual leader of Western christendom. The vision of the French school of spirituality passed almost unchallenged down to the twentieth century.

Seventeenth-century France became known for Jansenism and for devotional excess. Some French Catholics believed that it sufficed to be devoted to Mary alone in order to be saved. Pierre de Berulle (d. 1629), the founder of a society of priests known as the French Oratory, even went so far as to say that Mary's *fiat* in assenting to the incarnation is "much more powerful in its issue and effect than (the word) that God pronounced when creating the universe."[16]

Jean Eudes, also a member of the Oratory, wrote works on marian spirituality. He saw Mary as a spouse of the priest. At age sixty-seven he drew up a formal contract of marriage with her. He preferred to meditate on Christ in the womb of his mother, a devotion dear to de Berulle and the French school.

With Louis-Marie Grignon de Montfort (d. 1716), the French school reached its peak of marian devotion. De Montfort has been called the master *par excellence* of marian devotion. His best known work is *The True Devotion to the Blessed Virgin*.[17] He believed that it was more perfect not to approach God directly, but to go more humbly through a mediator. This was a rather Jansenist attitude, although the Jansenists themselves were certainly opposed to de Montfort. Small tokens of love for the Blessed Virgin, he said, were not sufficient for salvation. He therefore demanded a complete interior surrender to her so as to be entirely formed by her.

Such devotional teaching and practices as we have just seen when discussing de Berulle, Eudes, and de Montfort were often very dubious. Confraternities of the "slaves of Mary" bound themselves in spiritual slavery to Mary, wearing small chains about their necks or wrists as a sign of their bondage.[18] Some took a vow, even to martyrdom, to defend belief in the immaculate conception (which was not yet official Catholic doctrine). Popular manuals of devotion for an increasingly literate population were often filled with bizarre piety about Mary. This piety included such stories as that of Mary renewing her vows of victim and servant at age three[19] or enjoying the angelic light that showed her all the actions of Jesus' soul, while he was still in her womb.[20]

The Eighteenth Century

The eighteenth-century Enlightenment was a philosophical movement that rejected extrinsic authority in favor of the authority of reason. This movement, emphasizing freedom of inquiry, freedom of decision, and freedom of action, posed a serious crisis for Christianity, which, until then, had been the sole authority for determining what was true and what was not. Few Enlightenment thinkers had much use for what they saw to be extravagant superstitions of religion. Led by the popular writings of Voltaire, they dismissed apparitions as gullible offenses against reason. Even the church, increasingly restrained by secular power and tempted by enlightenment rationalism, lost interest in promoting the cult. Marian feasts were stricken from local church calendars, shrines fell into ruin, and excessive devotions were discouraged. During the French Revolution some churches removed their statues of Mary, and the statue of the goddess of reason was enthroned in Notre Dame cathedral in Paris. Marian literature ceased to exist, although popular devotion was catered to by sermons and by pamphlets put out by congregations particularly devoted to Mary. The Jesuits, promoters of the marian cult, were disbanded.

From the Nineteenth Century to Vatican II

The nineteenth century marked the beginning of the "Age of Mary." The republican ideals of the Revolution failed. Romanticism, an attitude of mind favorable to irrational influences, to emotional as well as mystical experiences, rejected the Enlightenment program. Marian teaching and devotion benefited from this new mood, and Catholic revival under the long-lived Pius IX signaled the rebirth of the marian cult. Alphonsus Liguori's book *The Glories of Mary* was one of the most popular works on marian devotions. For Liguori, Mary's role in this world was to raise up souls that had fallen from divine grace and to reconcile them to God, a role traditionally given to Christ. If God is angry with a sinner, he says, "Mary takes him under her protection, [and] withholds the avenging arm of her Son, and saves him."[21] The growing demand to have the doctrine of the immaculate conception officially defined signaled the need for official recognition of Mary. This led to its proclamation as dogma in 1854.

By the mid-century, apparitions of Mary were recorded all over Europe, especially in France: Paris in 1830, Rome in 1842, La Salette in 1846, Lourdes in 1858, Normandy in 1871, Knock, Ireland, in 1879. Both in popular preaching and in theological discussion Mary had become a more and more autonomous figure. She was no longer seen in the Trinitarian, christological, or ecclesial contexts within which the early Christians had seen her. There was an exaggerated emphasis given to our dependence on her. Certain interpretations of the devotion promulgated by Louis Grignon de Montfort became popular once more with the revival of marian spirituality, a spirituality that had declined in the age of the

Enlightenment. De Montfort's emphasis on praying "To Jesus through Mary" is a case in point here. Little attention was paid to Mary's own dependence on Christ.

The first sixty years of the twentieth century saw the continued importance of marian enthusiasm. Further apparitions were recorded: at Fatima in Portugal in 1917, and at Beauraing, Belgium, in 1932. Lay groups designed to carry out a marian-oriented apostolate led to the blossoming of marian confraternities and movements, strangely enough with a distinctly militant flavor. The Legion of Mary, founded in 1921, and the Blue Army, in 1947, are examples of such movements. The Legion of Mary is organized on the model of an army, its members promising to serve in this warfare, which is perpetually waged by the church against the world and its evil powers. Inspired by the spirituality of Grignon de Montfort, the legionary becomes a slave of Mary, committing absolutely everything to her.

In 1950, the promulgation of the dogma of the assumption marked another jewel in Mary's crown. Piety and theology kept pace with official documents. In René Laurentin's words, "never can enough honor be given to Mary." Rosemary Haughton, comparing present and medieval images of Mary, writes:

> the crowned and superb Queen of the older images, and even the gentle, vital and confident young Mother of medieval iconography, gave way to a meek, melancholy, and scarcely adult virgin, who during the nineteenth century, was allowed less and less bosom and no crown at all. Even Bernadette's vision at Lourdes of an irrepressibly lively and young but regal "Lady" was modified to meet the current requirement: tilted head, wilting body, resigned expression; and women, and most especially "religious" women, were required to identify with this model. Many did so, internalizing to such an extent that no other way of being devout could be imagined.[22]

The nineteenth century was the age of the suppressed woman, but Rosemary Haughton reminds us that the wilting and submissive Victorian lady on whom Mary was modeled, was really the last desperate effort of a lost cause.[23] It was also an age of very strong women; the Women's Suffrage Movement was a symbol of a changed consciousness and expectations that would continue to ask disturbing questions about gender privilege. Ivone Gebara and Maria Clara Bingemer add:

> At each new historical moment for Christians, the mystery of Mary unveils a different facet, one that deeply touches the needs of the poor and believing people...and places women in active participation on an equal basis with men....This perspective is not yet something achieved in our era, but it is being announced strongly and vigorously, and it brings life for the future.[24]

In this century, too, Mary has stood between heaven and earth, a quasi-divine being, and was exalted as the "Mediatrix of All Graces," "Co-redemptrix," "Mother of the Church." Catholic spirituality came close to divinizing Mary as a co-principal of redemption.

The Needs of Every Age

The beginnings of the marian cult are obscure. It has been explained as a deep psychological need for the worship of the mother. John Shinners agrees that some aspects of the veneration of Mary may be borrowed from pre-Christian earth-mother and fertility cults.[25] He is careful, however, not to rely only on psychological needs:

> Jungian psychologists locate the appeal of Mary in society's corporate need to express the archetypical feminine and maternal images of the collective unconscious. Freudians see in the cult a sublimation of male oedipal urges. All of these theories fail for various reasons.[26]

From both the devotional and doctrinal traditions, Mary has become known through history by hundreds of names, including: Mother, Virgin, Queen, Immaculate Conception, Our Lady of Mercy, of Sorrows, of Peace, of Perpetual Help, of the Highway, of the Rosary, of Chartres, Lourdes, Fatima, and Guadalupe. Every age tends to shape her according to its own needs. These manifestations of Mary tell us a lot about our own needs. They often tell us more about the church in any particular situation in history than about Mary herself.

Mary has been shaped largely by the imaginations of many generations of Christians and has adapted herself to the religious needs of the faithful in various times and places. The church has constantly turned to her to meet the ever-changing aspects of Christian discipleship. She has been its model in re-embodying in particular times, places, and cultures the love and justice of God. Because times and cultures vary, the challenge of Christian discipleship and the demands of radical living of the gospel also vary and can never be rigidly prescribed. Every age, therefore, unconsciously forms its image of Mary according to its own ideal.

The Cult of Mary and Its Influence on the Lives of Women

The marian tradition in the Roman Catholic church has had both liberating and oppressive effects on women. Among the liberating aspects, it is important to note that the marian tradition has kept the image of woman central to the process of salvation. Second, the centrality of the image of Mary in Catholicism points to a deep intuition that the deity cannot be adequately portrayed in images that describe God's activities only as creating, redeeming, and administering justice.[27] The tendency to apply quasi-divine attributes, such as co-redemptrix, to Mary is in itself a critique of this persistently controlling imaging of God throughout the long Christian tradition.

In terms of negative aspects, it is an interesting observation that in countries like the Philippines and Mexico where uncritical and emotionally charged marian devotions still flourish, women are not involved in any significant way in public or political life. The Philippine report to the recent World Conference on Women in Beijing, China, offers extensive data on the position of women in Philippine society and the few women elected to public office from 1986-1995. The two most influential of these during that period, Imelda Marcos and Corazon Aquino, derived their influence from their spouses. The report adds that women in the Philippines did take an unprecedented active role in the political upheaval of the last decade, but, "despite this, the number of women in elected posts is extremely low, reflecting the inequality of the sharing of power and decision making."[28] The churches in these and similar countries of Spanish Christian origin are not open to the full participation of women in public ministries.[29]

The confusions and exaggerations about Mary, conceptual and imaginative, reached their peak in the 1950s. Such was the situation on the eve of the Second Vatican Council.

Conclusion

The long history of marian piety nourished the popular religious imagination of the people through the centuries. We must be slow, therefore, to make superficial or hasty judgments about it, either in its popular preaching or devotional expressions, however bizarre some of these expressions may seem to us today. The simpler Catholic faithful, especially the poor and the deprived, have sought in Mary a strength that enabled them to interpret life, to feel accompanied and not abandoned, and to hope, no matter how bad the circumstances and tragedies of their lives.

It was the task of the Second Vatican Council to bring marian devotion within the limits of sound theology and practice. We will study the contributions of the council in Chapter Five.

Questions for Reflection and Discussion

1. Every age has unconsciously formed its own image of Mary according to its own needs. Trace the different emphases on mariology through the centuries and show how these emphases have met the needs of Christians in the different eras of history.

2. Images of God and Mary in the Middle Ages were influenced by both the spirituality and the feudal culture of European society. Discuss and illustrate with examples.

3. In the sixteenth century the reformers drastically rejected marian devotion. Why would some contemporary Protestant scholars contend that this was a mistake? What is your opinion?

4. Devotion to Mary in the history of the church has had both liberative and oppressive effects on women. List and discuss these effects. Is Mary still an ambiguous symbol today, especially for women? Why? Why not?

Suggestions for Further Reading

Grassi, Carolyn and Joseph. *Mary, Mother & Disciple: From the Scriptures to the Council of Ephesus.* Wilmington, DE: Michael Glazier, 1988, pp. 96-149.

Johnson, Elizabeth. "Saints and Mary," *Systematic Theology: Roman Catholic Perspectives,* eds. Francis S. Fiorenza and John P. Galvin. Dublin: Gill and Macmillan, 1992, pp. 467-501.

_____. "Marian Devotion in the Western Church," *Christian Spirituality: High Middle Ages and Reformation: An Encyclopedic History of the Religious Quest,* ed. Jill Raitt. New York: Crossroad, 1986, pp. 392-440.

Shinners, John R. "Mary and the People: The Cult of Mary and Popular Belief." *Mary: Woman of Nazareth,* ed. Doris Donnelly. New York: Paulist Press, 1989, pp. 161-186.

CHAPTER FIVE

MARY IN THE THEOLOGY
OF VATICAN II

Popular devotion that appeals to a wide audience frequently leads to distortions and abuses. As a result of such distortion, Mary has sometimes been placed on a par with Christ the redeemer in such a way that his unique mediatorship of redemption becomes superfluous. The excesses of popular belief, resulting in the figure of Mary assuming divine prerogatives, reached their peak on the eve of the Second Vatican Council.

The conciliar discussions offered a serious corrective to these excesses. The council reversed the tendency to promote a marian doctrine and devotion that isolated Mary from Christ and the rest of the church.

In tracing the council's emotional debate on Mary, we will note its emphasis on the centrality of Christ's mediatorship and on Mary's role in the mystery of Christ and the church. We will conclude with a discussion on postconciliar developments in marian theology.

Pre-Vatican II Mariology

The study of Mary's role in the mystery of salvation was vigorously pursued by mariologists during the century leading up to the Second Vatican Council. Theological writings on Mary were mostly done by specialist mariologists, whose reflections were often divorced from the rest of theology. Two main themes interested these theologians: Mary as "coredemptrix" and as "mediatrix" of all graces, themes that were concerned

with Mary's part in the redemption worked by her Son, and the application of the fruits of that redemption to humanity.

Mary's place in Christ's redemption had been a topic of discussion since
the second century. Through the centuries theology had reflected on her
cooperation with God's plan of salvation at the annunciation, the beginning of a life of commitment that finally ended in the sacrificial offering
of herself in union with her Son at the foot of the cross (John 19:25–28a).
This was the sacrificial offering that redeemed the human race.
Mariologists sought to understand what Mary's cooperation meant. Some
affirmed her immediate and approximate cooperation in the work of
redemption and suggested different ways by which she cooperated; others suggested her role lay in a subjective redemption alone.

The title "mediatrix" dates back to the fifteenth century. In the encyclical *Ad Diem Illum* Pius X stated:

> By this companionship in sorrow and suffering between the Mother
> and the Son, it has been allowed to the most august Virgin to be the
> most powerful mediatrix and advocate of the whole world with her
> Divine Son....Since Mary has been associated with Jesus Christ in
> the work of redemption, she merits for us what is called *de congruo*
> [by a title of appropriateness] those things which Christ merited *de
> condigno* [in justice], and she is the supreme minister of the distrib-
> ution of graces.[1]

The title of "co-redemptrix" was used in official statements under Pius
X, and employed again by Pius XI. In the teachings of the magisterium,
however, it was more common to speak of Mary's cooperation in our
redemption.

Conciliar Theology

Instead of a separate document on Mary, the Second Vatican Council
decided to include one chapter on her in the Dogmatic Constitution on
the Church (*Lumen Gentium*). It is Chapter 8, entitled "The Role of the
Blessed Virgin Mary, Mother of God, in the Mystery of Christ and the
Church." The very title of the chapter portrays Mary in an intimate relationship with her Son and his body the church. Yves Congar commented
that the preposition "in" of the title was of great ecumenical significance

since it favored a "sharing-oriented" rather than a "privilege-centered" approach to mariology.[2] Thus, the council ended marian theology's isolation and rooted it firmly in the mainstream of the truths of faith.

Influenced by an atmosphere of ecumenical sensitivity the council was now eager to stress the sole mediatorship of Christ. It is in this context of the whole church together, living and dead, and centered in Christ, that the Dogmatic Constitution on the Church places Mary. Its reflection on Mary must be understood within the constitution's central themes of christology, ecclesiology, and eschatology. A preface to this chapter notes that Mary is "one with all human beings in their need for salvation" while at the same time remaining a "pre-eminent and altogether singular member of the Church" (par. 53).

A cursory glance at *Lumen Gentium* shows the sequence of topics. Chapter 1, "The Mystery of the Church" begins with the proclamation, "Christ is the light of all nations." It is the radiance of this light that brightens the church, the assembly of all those who believe in Christ and witness to him in the world. In proclaiming the gospel, the church brings Christ's light to all peoples. In Chapter 2 the document discusses the church as the pilgrim people of God. The various functions of the episcopacy and pastors are spelled out in Chapter 3, followed by the responsibility of the laity in Chapter 4. The church's call to holiness is stressed in Chapter 5, and the different religious families within the church in Chapter 6. In Chapter 7 the eschatological nature of the pilgrim church and the union of the beloved dead with God invite us to look forward in hope, as we are signed with the Holy Spirit, "who is the pledge of our inheritance" (Ephesians 1:14). Finally, in Chapter 8, the constitution discusses the role of the Blessed Virgin Mary, "who occupies a place in the church which is highest after Christ and yet very close to us."[3] The constitution situates her in the midst of the communion of saints, those whose prayer and example in heaven give courage and hope to the pilgrim church on earth.

The Conciliar Debate

While the theological commission of the council had already voted by a two-thirds majority to include the text on Mary in the document, it was decided to ask the council fathers for a general vote.[4] Cardinal Santos of Manila was named to speak for a separate text, and Cardinal Koenig of

Vienna for inclusion. Santos represented those who emphasized Mary's preeminence over all under Christ and her instrumental role in bringing the church into being. He argued that the document on the church was too short to do justice to a schema on Mary; he asked the council to provide a complete doctrine of faith about her. Cardinal Koenig, on the other hand, was concerned that a separate document would create the false impression that Vatican II intended to define a new marian dogma. Integrating marian teaching into the council's doctrine on the church, he argued, should place Mary in the context of the council's central teaching. This would help to overcome the theological and devotional excesses that resulted from unduly isolating Mary from the mystery of Christ and the church.

Michael Novak's critique during the second session of the council shows how Mary became the key symbol in the conciliar struggle between traditionalists and progressives.[5] According to Novak, the traditionalists (who pressed for a separate document on Mary) ignored the social and political implications of the gospel when they separated personal devotion from public life and linked marian devotions to a refuge from the conflicts of history. On the emotional conciliar debate on marian piety Novak says:

The man of history has little time for such devotions, such attitudes....In effect it insists that men withdraw from the real, concrete daily work of human progress. Not by accident does non-historical orthodoxy have a stronger hold on women than on men, especially in the lower classes; these are the ones whose lives have changed least since the late Middle Ages.[6]

In a summary of Novak's critique, Anne Carr comments:

Novak linked withdrawal from the problems of the world, focus on personal sins and misdemeanours, intellectual ignorance of the biblical and liturgical foundations of Christianity, fear of change and anti-communism. This spirituality was especially prevalent in Spain and Italy...countries whose class structures remained rigid, and whose political power groups have a great stake in keeping the energy of the church involved in private devotions to Mary and the saints.[7]

According to Novak, those who favored including the text on Mary within the document on the church were those "who labored at a theology of the Word of God, of the liturgy, of social action, of the return to the earlier traditions of Christianity."[8]

After long and emotional debates, with fears that this issue might even split the council, a very narrow majority vote, 1114 to 1074, went for inclusion. The document placed Mary within the wider framework of the whole economy of salvation. Without detracting from her preeminence and uniqueness in salvation history, the council related her to Christ in a dependent and subordinate way that does not separate her from solidarity with the rest of the redeemed members of his body. The authors were cautiously placing Mary in an auxiliary relationship to Christ, thus helping to diminish the marian excesses of the preconciliar period. The very graces and prerogatives that unite Mary so closely with Christ our redeemer bring her into an intimate union with each one of us, for just as Christ cannot be separated from his body, the church, so neither can Mary be so closely associated with Christ's redemptive incarnation without being closely associated with all the members.

On the eve of the council, there was some hope that a new marian dogma would be defined, either of Mary as co-redemptrix or as mediatrix of all graces. But the council's decision against a separate document placed her in privileged and splendid isolation no longer. As a preeminent and singular member of the church, she is the one who heard the Word of God and acted upon it (Luke 11:28), and thus became the Mother of the Son of God. Yet she remains at the same time a daughter of Adam and Eve and "one with all human beings in their need for salvation."[9]

While the council fathers specify the annunciation and Mary at Calvary, two events in the life of Mary stressed by earlier mariologists, they are careful to include the whole life of Mary:

The Blessed Virgin Mary was eternally predestined, in conjunction with the incarnation of the divine Word, to be the Mother of God....She conceived, brought forth, and nourished Christ. She presented Him to the Father in the temple, and was united with Him in suffering as he died on the cross. In an utterly singular way she cooperated by her obedience, faith, hope, and burning charity in the Savior's work of restoring supernatural life to souls.[10]

Throughout the document there is emphasis both on Mary's motherhood, the means by which Jesus our redeemer entered the world, and on her continuous response to God's call throughout her life. It was "her pilgrimage of faith"[11] that finally led her to the cross.

Christ's Mediatorship

Because preconciliar theology emphasized Mary as mediatrix of all graces, the council was careful to place her mediation within the framework of Christ and the church. It is an unnecessary polarization to set Mary over against her Son, as some Protestants and Catholics have done. Where Mary's role is central, Jesus' role is distorted, for she distracts from the centrality of his redeeming mission. The council gave repeated emphasis to Christ as our one mediator drawing all believers to himself.[12] He is the one priest of the New Covenant whose priesthood is shared by all the people of God. Before the council fathers spoke of Mary's mediation, they stressed the unique mediation of Christ. They chose a passage from 1 Timothy that emphasizes the universality of salvation: "For there is one God, and there is one mediator between God and humankind, Christ Jesus, himself human, who gave himself as a ransom for all" (1 Timothy 2:5–6). Mary's role as our mother does not diminish Christ's unique mediation; rather it reveals its effectiveness:

> The maternal duty of Mary towards men in no way obscures or diminishes this unique mediation of Christ, but rather shows its power. For all the saving influences of the Blessed Virgin on men originate, not from some inner necessity, but from the divine pleasure. They flow forth from the superabundance of the merits of Christ, rest on his mediation, depend entirely on it, and draw all their power from it. In no way do they impede the immediate union of the faithful with Christ. Rather, they foster this union.[13]

When the document states that the church invokes Mary as mediatrix, it is quick to add that this title neither takes from nor adds anything to the dignity and efficacy of Christ, the one mediator. With this conviction firmly in view, the special reverence with which believers venerate Mary's memory and which has taken diverse forms in various cultures should be encouraged.

With the heart of a mother, Mary continuously prays for those who are still on the way and beset with difficulties. For this reason she is called upon in the church [not by the church, as the original text had said] under many titles such as Auxiliatrix and Mediatrix.... Christ is at the center, believers have immediate union with him, and all are empowered by him in the Spirit.[14]

Mary's intercession is not viewed as interposed between humans and a wrathful Christ. Rather, she is caught up into his unique mediatorship on our behalf. Anne Carr comments:

Thus might be allayed Protestant Christians' fears about Catholic tendencies to divinise Mary, especially in the nineteenth and twentieth centuries, in the statements of Pius IX, X, XI, and XII, and so to remove her from salvation in Christ alone. There is a minimum number of citations of papal pronouncements and an abundance of biblical and patristic references, especially from the Greek fathers, thus recognizing Eastern Christianity's ancient and continuing devotion to Mary as the Mother of God. Yet nothing truly Catholic is left out: the dogmas of the Immaculate Conception and the Assumption are affirmed and devotion to Mary is encouraged.[15]

Although Chapter 8 of the Dogmatic Constitution reflects the transitional nature of many of the council documents, its approach is essentially biblical, christocentric, ecclesiological, ecumenical, and pastoral. It moves away from a preconciliar mariology that centered on Mary and her privileges and fostered marian titles and dogmas. The council fathers wish to remind us of the danger of superficial sentiment. They emphasize Mary as the preeminent member of the church and the model of its pilgrim life of faith. While the dominant theme in this brief chapter of *Lumen Gentium* is Mary as type and model of the church, it is interesting to note that she is never addressed as "Mother of the Church."

While this constitution is a serious corrective to certain past emphases, it is unfortunate that it did not situate discussion on Mary within the signs of the times. There was no dialogue with the modern world, which is the key to the spirit of the council; guidelines for an authentic devotion to Mary were not suggested. Feminist theologians are quick to remind us that the council continued to praise Mary as the woman in the service of others, of God, of Christ, of the church, and of redemption; she has no theological meaning of her own.[16] Women know how harmful such interpretations have been for them for centuries. As the inferior "other," autonomous personhood has been beyond their grasp, and Mary has been used once more, they say, to reinforce this view. Besides, uncritical readings of biblical texts continue to use the Eve–Mary typology. It was left to the postconciliar period to discover an authentic marian theology for our day.

In the Aftermath of the Council

Mariology suffered a decline in interest after the council. The long marian silence for some years afterwards led many to express the fear that the Blessed Virgin Mary was being deliberately downgraded.

One important reason for the declining interest in Mary was that theologians were drawn to explore new perspectives in major areas of ecclesiology, christology, and biblical studies. They were also involved in the implementation of the liturgical changes recommended by the council. Vatican II's concern for the modern world, its reemphasis on the scriptural foundations of faith, and its call to the social gospel seemed to have temporarily checked the flow of marian piety.

In preconciliar days, the rosary, novenas, and other marian devotions had come to be placed on a par with the Eucharist and the other sacraments. Now with the recovery of the bible and the new emphasis on the liturgy in the vernacular, rosaries and novenas began to disappear. Mary, and devotion to her, began to be placed in relation to Christ and the Eucharist. While the marian emphasis in the liturgy began to diminish, however, other forms of marian piety were emerging in the form of pilgrimages to sites of apparitions. (We will discuss this phenomenon in greater detail in the Appendix.) Since 1981 an estimated seven to eight million people have visited the pilgrimage site of Medjugorje in Yugoslavia. What this reality is telling us about people's efforts of bringing faith and life together needs to be discerned in the light of Vatican II.

The revitalized interest in Mary in more recent years differs significantly from the old mariology. Theologians are now reluctant to be called mariologists. The council, in trying to correct earlier deviations, such as seeing Mary as a buffer between Jesus and us, affirmed that "Mary in virtue of her mission and by the merits of her Son...far surpasses all creatures both in heaven and on earth."[17] Mariology has been absorbed into christology, and it is with Christ as the focal point that Mary is now studied. In a compact formulation the council states that "Mary occupies a place in the church which is the highest after Christ and closest to us."[18]

Just as our forebears in the faith developed practices of devotion for their times, the postconciliar church needs to adapt inherited practices, or develop new ones, to honor Mary in our times. In *Redemptoris Mater,*[19] Pope John Paul II speaks often of Mary's journey of faith. We need to keep this in mind as we reflect on the very human Mary who moved from unbelief to belief, who experienced the concern of a mother over her son's unorthodox activities, and who knew suffering at his death.

Postconciliar Developments

1. Marialis Cultus

It was left to Pope Paul VI's apostolic exhortation *Marialis Cultus,* published ten years after the council, to begin to develop a contemporary mariology that integrated the concerns of Vatican II's Pastoral Constitution on the Church in the Modern World with the theological and ecumenical emphases of *Lumen Gentium. Marialis Cultus* must be acknowledged as an important contribution to the postconciliar discussion about marian devotion. It stresses that devotion to Mary must find "its origin and effectiveness from Christ, find its complete expression in Christ and lead through Christ in the Spirit to the Father."[20] Devotion to Mary, it states, must be rooted in the great themes of salvation history; it should be shaped by the feasts of the liturgical year; be ecumenically sensitive, especially to the centrality of Christ; and be attuned to the historical and cultural situations of time and place. The pope is concerned that:

> Certain practices of piety that not so long ago seemed suitable for expressing the religious sentiment of individuals and communities seem today inadequate or unsuitable because they are linked with social and cultural patterns of the past.[21]

He also warns that:

> Certain aspects of the image of Mary found in popular writings are

not connected with the Gospel image of Mary, nor with the doctrinal data which have been made explicit through a slow and conscientious process of drawing from revelation.[22]

Paul VI encourages episcopal conferences, local churches, and religious communities to take the initiative in carefully revising expressions of marian piety[23] and offers a firm reminder that:

> The Second Vatican Council has already authoritatively denounced both the exaggeration of content and form, which even falsifies doctrine, and...certain devotional deviations...which substitutes reliance on merely external practices for serious commitment.[24]

He notes the changed situation of women in contemporary society, which greatly influences marian piety.[25] Women today are co-responsible for the running of the family, and new positions in politics and public life are opening up to them. Besides, they have access to a whole range of employment options and to new possibilities in scientific research and higher studies that bring them out of the restricted surroundings of the home. In the context of these experiences, women have become disenchanted with historical representations of Mary that encourage only docility, humility, and self-effacement. Pope Paul exhorts theologians to examine these difficulties carefully.[26]

There is a strong emphasis on Mary's "active and responsible consent" for women who participate in decision making in the community.[27] The pope also offers what he calls a "pleasant surprise" for women, when he stresses that not only was Mary not a timidly submissive woman but, on the contrary, "a woman of strength, who experienced poverty and suffering, flight and exile."[28] This offers new hope to those who suggest that marian devotion is empty of moral significance today, and especially to contemporary women who are struggling to realize their own dignity. Finally, Mary is offered as a model disciple for both women and men who work for justice and for freeing the oppressed, who assist the needy and who actively witness to the "love that builds up Christ in people's hearts."[29]

2. *Redemptoris Mater*

Pope John Paul II's encyclical *Redemptoris Mater* was written in 1987
on the feast of the Annunciation to initiate the Marian Year. The Marian
Year was meant to celebrate the two thousandth anniversary of the birth
of the Blessed Virgin Mary. It was also meant to be a preparatory celebration for the coming two thousandth commemoration of the birth of Jesus.
The encyclical states its purpose: "a new and more careful reading of what
the council said about the Blessed Virgin Mary, Mother of God, in the
mystery of Christ and of the Church."[30] It has a different purpose than
that of *Marialis Cultus*, thirteen years earlier. Its focus is doctrinal rather
than devotional, although doctrinal reflection is intended to lead to a
renewal of devotion.

While the Second Vatican Council indicated the direction theological
inquiry should take, *Redemptoris Mater* took up some of the issues still left
open after Vatican II. At the council, as we have seen, statements about
Mary's mediation were seen at best to be a compromise. *Redemptoris Mater*
stresses the "singularity and uniqueness of Mary's place in the Mystery of
Christ,"[31] and her "active and exemplary presence in the life of the
Church."[32] Her mediation is mediation in Christ. Second, her mediation
is linked to her motherhood, which distinguishes it from the mediation
of all other creatures. Finally it is a mediation *within* and not *from above*
the church, which embraces the whole of humanity.[33]

In the pope's concern for ecumenism, he makes mention of the coming of Christianity to Russia one thousand years ago. In this context the
title *Theotokos*, Mary the Mother of God, venerated both in the East and
the West, becomes an ecumenical bond of no small importance for him.[34]
The pope lists the icons of the Virgin by which Eastern Christians contemplate her faith and glory, and he prays hopefully that the symbol of
Mary, and the wealth of praise that reaches her from the entire church,
will hasten the day when the church will once more breathe fully with her
"two lungs," the East and the West.[35]

While the pope makes mention of the "free and active ministry of
women,"[36] he makes no comment on the changed experience of women
in today's society, as Paul VI did in *Marialis Cultus*. Rather, the pope sees
woman as capable "of self-offering love," "of bearing the greatest sorrows,"
and "of limitless fidelity and tireless devotion to work."[37] These are well-
meaning, but destructive images for women who are struggling to realize

their full personhood. Women also take issue with the belief that Mary's privileges as intermediary seem to have been given to her because she was a pure and passive vessel.

3. Behold Your Mother

In their pastoral letter *Behold Your Mother* (1973), the American bishops are sensitively aware that Mary, imaged as the new Eve, had been used by church fathers to equate all other women with the old Eve.[38] In avoiding this image of Mary, the bishops focus instead upon Mary as a model of liberation. In the earlier drafts of their pastoral letter *Partners in the Mystery of Redemption,* the U.S. bishops also are aware of the troubling image that many past depictions of Mary convey. They also know that many women are unhappy with images that represent Mary as a woman valued chiefly for her virginity and maternity, and confined to domestic and familial roles.

In *Behold Your Mother* the bishops emphasize that "the dignity which Christ's redemption won for all women was fulfilled uniquely in Mary as a model of all feminine freedom."[39] The imaging of Mary as a prophetic woman of liberation bears meaning for the whole church today. As church, all men and women are challenged to live the Magnificat song of the church. Active hope in God's power can transform the world and the church into a community of liberty and justice for all. The bishops also point out that:

> Our faith does not seek out new gospels, but leads us to know the excellence of the Mother of God and moves us to filial love toward our Mother and to the imitation of her virtues.[40]

Conclusion

The decision at Vatican II to include Mary within the document on the church heralded a significant shift in marian theology. This was an important step in a church that, on the eve of the council, came close to divinizing Mary as a co-principal of redemption. In the ecumenically sensitive atmosphere of the council, Christ's sole mediatorship was stressed continuously. Mary is no longer to be considered in splendid isolation but in her theological role within the community of believers. She is the preeminent member of the church, its model for the church's pilgrim life of faith.

In contrast to the conciliar document, both *Marialis Cultus* and *Redemptoris Mater* clearly situate the discussion on Mary much more clearly within the social and cultural climate of the times. While both of these papal letters were concerned to take up some of the issues left open by the council, it was the theology of liberation, and feminist theology in particular, that issued the radical challenge to reread the significance of Mary for our times. These theologies suggest that we focus on Mary as a prophet of God, committed to realizing God's plan of salvation in history. The U.S. bishops, echoing the insights of liberation theology, focus on a prophetic image of Mary, the woman committed to the liberation of the poor from the social injustices from which they suffer. It is from the context of the reality of women's lives, however, that feminist theologians offer a new starting point for a theology of Mary. This will be the focus of our discussion in Chapter Seven.

Questions for Reflection and Discussion

1. Describe the situation of preconciliar mariology immediately before the Second Vatican Council.

2. Discuss the importance of the Second Vatican Council's debate on Mary for ecclesiology and for offering a serious corrective to preconciliar marian theology.

3. Why did the decision of the council to include the Mary text within the Constitution on the Church, rather than write a separate document on Mary, herald a significant shift in marian theology?

4. Do you agree that the documents *Redemptoris Mater* and *Marialis Cultus* have contributed significantly to the postconciliar discussion on Mary? What are their strengths and failings?

Suggestions for Further Reading

Carr, Anne. "Mary in the Mystery of the Church," in *Mary According to Women*, ed. Carol Frances Jegen. Kansas City: Leaven Press, 1985, pp. 5-32.

———. "Mary, Model of Faith," in *Mary, Woman of Nazareth*, ed. Doris Donnelly. New York: Paulist Press, 1989, pp. 7-24.

Hines, Mary. "Mary and the Prophetic Mission of the Church," *Journal of Ecumenical Studies*, 28:2, Spring 1991, pp. 281-298.

John Paul II. *Redemptoris Mater*, 1987.

Paul VI. *Marialis Cultus*, 1974.

CHAPTER SIX

THE TRADITION OF MARIAN SYMBOLS

Marian Symbols

In the preceding chapters we have noted the tremendous power of the symbol of Mary as it has captured the Christian imagination through the centuries both in popular devotion and theological reflection. The present upsurge of interest in marian devotions and sites of pilgrimage is evidence that the marian tradition communicates a deep symbolic truth. Mary has become, as Elizabeth Johnson has suggested, "that corporate personality who embodies symbolically the past, present, and future of Christian life."[1] This chapter is concerned with the power of religious symbols, and of marian symbols in particular. But first, let us inquire briefly into the meaning of metaphors and symbols.

The Power of Metaphor and Symbol

Sallie McFague and other contemporary theologians have recently sought to develop new metaphors to express the mystery of God and the God-human relationship. McFague defines a metaphor as "seeing one thing *as* something else, pretending 'this' is 'that' because we do not know how to think or talk about 'this,' so we use 'that' as a way of saying something about it."[2] Metaphorical language shocks and disturbs because it brings together dissimilar ideas, such as the buried treasure and the kingdom of God. While the metaphor involves an interchange of meaning between two terms, it emphasizes some details while suppressing others. As Regina Coll succinctly states:

> Each term says something about the other; meaning is transferred in both directions. We think new thoughts about each of the terms, even though we are primarily interested in the principal term. The metaphor "War is hell," for example, tells us something about the principal term, war, but it also implies something about our understanding of hell.[3]

A symbol, on the other hand, bridges two realities and brings them together in a new unity. It is a "complex of gestures, sounds, images, and/or words that evoke, invite, and persuade participation in that to which they refer."[4] Its very dynamism leads us into deeper reality through a sharing in the meaning that the symbol itself offers. In the words of Paul Ricoeur, "the symbol gives rise to thought [and] is balanced by an equal emphasis on thought's need to return to its rich base in symbol."[5] It is therefore an apt vehicle of religious meaning and opens us up to mystery.

It was the Protestant theologian Langdon Gilkey[6] who noted that Catholicism has had a continuing experience, unequalled in other forms of Western Christianity, of the presence of God and of grace, mediated through symbols, to the entire course of ordinary human life. David Tracy likewise notes that symbols inspire the imagination to concentrate so many ideas "that they arouse more thought than can be expressed in a concept determined by words,"[7] and Anne Carr stresses that symbolic truth is more, not less, than truth that can be historically verified.[8]

Liberation theologians, knowing that societies are changed more by symbols than by concepts, have shown how oppressed urban and rural Christians in Latin America have accorded privileged place in their scriptural reflections to the symbols of the Exodus, Jesus the Liberator, and the Magnificat. These traditional Christian symbols are brought directly into conversation with the lives of the poor.

To regain the effective and directive power that many symbols, and the marian symbols in particular, have lost for us, we need to allow some of them to die, others to emerge, the rest to be subjected to a critical reinterpretation. But substitution and change take time, for people are slow to let go of the familiar, to which they are emotionally attached. They are even more reluctant to part with religious symbols that have accumulated layer upon layer of meaning for them and that have gripped their allegiance over a long period of time.

Christian Symbols and the Culture that Gave Them Birth

No one creates images of Mary (or of God). Like all religious images they are born and die in a culture because of complex reasons.[9] Christian culture is highly patriarchal, and a close look at its structures of domination can show how they have shaped our religious thinking and biased the whole range of theological symbols. Nowhere is this more obvious than in our language about God.

In a certain structure of divine-human relationships, men possess the image of God primarily; women relate to God only secondarily. Paul (despite Galatians 3:28) reaffirms this patriarchal order of relationships in 1 Corinthians 11:3–7:

> But I want you to understand that the head of every man is Christ, the head of a woman is her husband, and the head of Christ is God.... For a man ought not to cover his head, since he is the image and glory of God; but woman is the glory of man.

Theology must critique the well-internalized, but no longer justifiable image given to women by church and society. In doing so it must examine the metaphors, symbols, models, and language that support these hierarchical, dualistic, and static ways of expressing the relationship between God and the world, and ourselves and the world. Ancient myths identifying woman with chaos, darkness, matter, and sin echo clearly in Christian interpretations of concupiscence (well-entrenched in the classical interpretation of original sin), of sexuality as contaminating, and, therefore, of woman as temptress, as danger, and as symbol of sin.

It is in this context that marian theology tries to understand the symbolic power of the changing image of Mary from the early centuries of Christianity to our own times, and its influence on the lives of women. Nietzsche has reminded us that "what we call truth are worn-out metaphors, which have become powerless to affect the senses."[10] Some of our traditional marian metaphors are well worn-out. Two such weary examples are the Eve–Mary and the New Adam–New Eve parallelisms.

We will now examine them both and discuss their historical influence on the long tradition of marian spirituality, paying particular attention to the consequences of these images for the lives of women.

The Eve–Mary Parallelism

The Eve–Mary parallelism is one of the most basic themes of the marian tradition. The contrasting of Mary to Eve had appeared as early as the first half of the second century and was never lost sight of again. While it is difficult to establish its origin, it is suggested that it was the parallel drawn in Romans 5:14 between Adam and Christ that inspired this theme, which became a favorite subject of patristic preaching. Walter Burghardt, the noted mariologist, writes that "the Eve–Mary analogy is the first genuine [!] insight of the patristic age with respect to Our Lady."[11] Eve and Mary are contrasted in terms of disobedience and obedience, unbelief and faith, death and life.

The famous *Protoevangelium*, "I will put enmity between you and the woman, and between your seed and her seed; he will bruise your head, and you shall bruise his heel" (Genesis 3:15), is also known as "the first good news." In Roman Catholic mariology this passage has been understood as a foreshadowing of Mary's co-redemptive role in the plan of God's salvation. Because the first Eve obeyed the serpent, she brought forth disobedience and death. The image of the woman crushing the head of the serpent reinforced the mariological understanding of Genesis 3:15 in the Western church. (The pronoun "he," which refers to the collective offspring or seed, was wrongly translated as "she," and given an exclusively literal marian sense.) Contemporary scholarship, however, realizes that the early church used the Genesis 3:15 passage in an accommodated sense,[12] and that in its original meaning it does not refer to Mary. In the classical exegesis of Genesis 3, Eve is characterized as the origin of sin. "In this way the anthropological and ethical dissimilarity of the sexes was given an exegetical and theological foundation."[13]

A sharp opposition is built between Mary the obedient and faithful woman and Eve the temptress and sinner. While Justin Martyr, Irenaeus, and Tertullian develop this symbolism with great embellishment, it is Irenaeus who stamps the idea on the mind of Christendom.[14] Justin concludes that Mary's cooperation with God contrasted sharply with the effects of Eve's seduction by Satan:

[The Son of God] became man through the Virgin, that the disobedience caused by the serpent might be destroyed in the same way in which it had originated. For Eve, while a virgin incorrupt, conceived the word that proceeded from the serpent, and brought forth disobedience and death. But the Virgin Mary was filled with faith and joy when the Angel Gabriel told her the glad tidings that the Spirit of the Lord would come upon her...and she answered: "Be it done unto me according to thy word."[15]

Irenaeus, perhaps the first theologian of the Virgin Mary, explains that the complicated knot fashioned of Eve's disobedience is untied by Mary's obedience:

Just as Eve, wife of Adam yes, yet still a virgin...became by her disobedience the cause of death for herself and the whole human race, so Mary too, espoused yet a virgin, became by her obedience the cause of salvation for herself and the whole human race....And so it was that the knot of Eve's disobedience was loosed by Mary's obedience. For what the virgin Eve bound fast by her refusal to believe, this the Virgin Mary unbound by her belief.[16]

A parallel passage in Irenaeus, one that Burghardt describes as "equally impressive," is worth citing in full:

For, as Eve was seduced by the utterance of an angel to flee God after disobeying his word, so Mary by the utterance of an angel had the glad tidings brought to her, that she should bear God in obedience to His word. And whereas Eve had disobeyed God, Mary was persuaded to obey God, that the Virgin Mary might become patroness of the virgin Eve. And as the human race was sentenced to death by means of a virgin, by means of a virgin is it delivered. A virgin's disobedience is balanced by a virgin's obedience.[17]

The same essential ideas—virginity, disobedience, and death, balanced by virginity, obedience, and life—are emphasized by Tertullian. Like Justin Martyr and Irenaeus, he believed that "what had been lost through one sex might by the same sex be restored and saved."[18] In addressing women he asks them: "Do you realize that you are each an Eve? The curse of God on this sex of yours lives on even in our times. Guilty you must bear its hardships."[19]

Jerome considered it an honor for a woman to be thought of as a man. Speaking to Lucinus about Theodora he says: "She has become your sister, has changed from woman to man, from subject to equal."[20] Again he adds that "as long as a woman is for birth and children, she is different from man as body is from soul. But when she wishes to serve Christ more than the world, then she will cease to be a woman, and will be called man."[21]

It would be difficult to understand the contrast between the veneration of Mary and the disgust of the female body in these writings, if we did not recall that it was commonplace in ancient thought to identify women with the flesh and men with the spirit, and to depict women as inevitably lower than men. St. Ambrose gives the source of the word *vir* (male) as *animi virtus* (strength of soul) and of the word *mulier* (woman) as *mollities mentis* (softness of mind).

Related to the symbol that describes Mary as the New Eve is that of the New Adam–New Eve. Christ the redeemer is the New Adam; the church, the new Eve, is his helpmate in the work of salvation. Both Ambrose and Augustine describe Mary and the church as virgins and mothers. Christ is cast in the preeminent role of divine partner; the human partner, Mary or the church, is cast in a childbearing role. Mary gives birth to Christ, the head, whose members, the church, are born in the Spirit. This androcentric system from the order of creation is transposed into the order of redemption. Kari Børresen shows that "the use of the New Adam–New Eve theme for nuptial symbolism rests on the patriarchal assumption that marriage is a union between two unequal partners."[22] But in today's world androcentricism is slowly breaking down so that this symbolism is gradually becoming an anachronism.

The insights of the fathers of the church, especially Justin, Irenaeus, and Tertullian, continued after Nicea in both East and West so that witnesses to the Eve–Mary parallelism, such as Jerome's well known phrase "death through Eve, life through Mary," follow one another "in an endless wave, across the whole of the Latin Middle Ages down to our own time."[23]

The scholastics continued this warped view of female sexuality. Thomas Aquinas adds: "Woman is an occasional and incomplete being…a misbegotten male. It is unchangeable that woman is destined to live under man's influence and has no authority from her Lord."

The work of the inquisitors and witch hunters could be legitimated by the negative views of women that find expression in the Eve–Mary typology. In the *Malleus Maleficarum,* the handbook on the persecution of witches written by two Dominicans in 1486, witchcraft is explicitly linked to the authors' perception of the inferiority of women's nature:

> Since women are feebler both in mind and body, it is not surprising that they should come under the spell of witchcraft. For as regards intellect, or the understanding of spiritual things, they seem to be of a different nature from men…But the natural reason is that she is more carnal than a man, as is clear from her many carnal abominations. And it should be noted that there was a defect in the formation of the first woman, since she was formed from a bent rib, that is, a rib of the breast which is bent as it were in a contrary direction to a man. And since through this defect she is an imperfect animal, she always deceives.[24]

In more recent times, when the immaculate conception of the Blessed Virgin Mary was proclaimed a dogma of faith on December 8, 1854, by the constitution *Ineffabilis Deus,* Pius IX compared Mary with Eve before she had "fallen." He then went on to describe her as a "lily among thorns" and "incorruptible wood." To acclaim Mary as a "lily among thorns" as the pope did is not very affirming for the thorns, for thorns by their very nature can never become lilies. And in describing her as "incorruptible wood" he seemed to insinuate that the rest of the wood is corruptible.

Vatican II, quoting Irenaeus and Jerome, again used the Eve–Mary typology in describing Mary as "the mother of the living."[25] Later, the Eve–Mary theme is mentioned in the context of the Mary–Church typology: "the New Eve who put her trust…not in the ancient serpent but in the messenger of God."[26] And most recently, in the apostolic letter *Mulieris Dignitatem,* Pope John Paul II's long reflection on the Eve–Mary analogy concludes that "in Mary Eve discovers the nature of the true dignity of woman, of feminine humanity."[27]

A Critique of the Eve–Mary Parallelism

In critiquing the long tradition of marian symbols, we must also examine the dominant culture out of which they have emerged, as well as the governing ideologies out of which the culture is living. Feminist scholars suggest that the Eve–Mary symbolism is one that ought to die. To exalt Mary at Eve's expense is to do so at the expense of all women. To place her on a pedestal as the holy virgin and mother and contrast her with the sinful Eve, the symbol of all ordinary women, makes it difficult to bridge the gap between the ordinary woman and Mary.[28] Donal Flanagan spells out the consequences of singling out Mary as the New Eve or New Woman:

> A price had to be paid for this singling out and the price was the identifying of all other women with the first Eve as fickle, unreliable, morally inferior beings in their natural condition. This dichotomization…the process by which the male divides woman by projecting two separate and contradictory symbols of her, did not begin with Christianity.[29] Rather the Christian marian tradition in due time produced its own dichotomization in Eve/Mary terms. This allowed the Christian male to project all his respect, honor, love onto one ideal, otherworldly woman, Mary, and thereby to salve his conscience for the actual subjection and low estate he allowed to real women in his patriarchal male-dominated world.

Mary *alone of all her sex* is uniquely holy and pure and becomes the great exception. It is in this context that virginity was interpreted as the resurrected life of the gospel whereby women were freed from the twofold curse on Eve (Genesis 3:16), the sorrows of childbearing, and male domination. In choosing virginity, women become spiritual men and rise above their femininity, often a symbol of moral danger and weakness.

Projecting the negative "seductive" Eve attributes on to other women does not help us to focus clearly on the solidarity of the whole human race, both women and men, in sin and grace. Elizabeth Johnson notes that "the denigration of women became the shadow side of the glorification of Mary in the early centuries of the church."[30] A well-established example of this problem is the "Madonna–whore syndrome," which allows men "to love and respect their ideal woman in Mary, but to ignore or dominate women with impunity and immunity even from the searchings of their own conscience."[31]

Because a system of domination has biased the whole range of theological symbols, traditional marian symbols such as Mary the New Eve, and the New Adam–New Eve typology have functioned, however unconsciously, to keep women oppressed. Women concerned about sexual identity, personal growth, and intellectual and social achievement must necessary reject such demeaning images.

The Eve–Mary typology can still be found at work in our culture, distorting our image of woman to one extreme or the other—deceitful seducer or lofty image of purity—and leaving us with the impression, spoken or unspoken, that women can't be trusted to do some things as well as men can. While today few would use the blatant language of *Malleus Maleficarum,* this typology, still very much alive in official church thought, as the recent *Catechism of the Catholic Church* attests, may have more to do with the prohibition against women in ordained ministry than the church can even realize or admit. We are still wary of the dangerous daughters of Eve! In *Behold Your Mother* (1973) the U. S. bishops avoided altogether the image of Mary as the new Eve and called her instead the model of feminine freedom. It is to be hoped that other church documents will follow the same path, but so far *Behold Your Mother* remains an exception.

The Suppression of the Feminine in Christianity

Contemporary studies in marian theology are examining the correlation between the decline in the influence of the feminine in Christianity and the corresponding growth in the cult of Mary. In Greco-Roman Christianity, probably because of the dangers of Gnosticism, the biblical images of God as female were soon suppressed within the doctrine of God. God as Wisdom, *Hokmah* or *Sophia* in Greek, a feminine form, was translated by Christianity into the *Logos* concept of Philo, which is masculine and was defined as the Son of God. The *Shekinah,* the theology of God's mediating presence as female, was de-emphasized; and God's Spirit, *Ruah,* a feminine noun in Hebrew, becomes neuter when translated into *Pneuma* in Greek. The Vulgate translates it into Latin as masculine, *Spiritus.* God's Spirit, *Ruah,* which at the beginning of creation brings forth abundant life in the waters, now makes the womb of Mary fruitful.

The challenge to theology today is to recover the richness of this tradition. In spite of the reality of the consoling, healing aspects of divine activity, the dominant patriarchal tradition has prevailed, resulting in seeing the female as the passive recipient of God's creation; and the female is expressed in nature, church, soul, and finally Mary as the prototype of redeemed humanity.

In the second century the exercise of authority in the church shifted from a charismatic and communal model, based on spiritual giftedness and economic resources, to patriarchal leadership restricted to the male heads of households.[32] Gradually this led to the relegation of women's leadership to marginal positions, and while leading women were still permitted to teach, their teaching was now restricted to the sphere of women.[33] The pastoral epistles (1 Timothy, 2 Timothy, Titus) stress obedience and submission to those in authority. Just as wives (Titus 2:5), children (1 Timothy 3:4), and slaves (Titus 2: 9) must be submissive within the patriarchal household, so they must observe their subordinate role within the community. In such a short time the understanding of female inferiority became so engrained that the negative Pauline and deutero-Pauline attitudes toward women prevailed over the more liberating attitude of Galatians 3:27–28.

At work here is the influence of Gnostic dualism that defines femaleness in relation to maleness: "Maleness is the subject, the divine, the absolute; femaleness is the opposite or the complementary 'other.'"[34] This cultural pattern of subordination was reinforced by the Pauline metaphors of head and body as well as of bridegroom and bride (2 Corinthians 11:3). This affected the relationship between Christ and the church, for the church or bride became totally dependent and submissive to her head, the bridegroom.

Correcting the Distortions in the Tradition

It may come as a surprise to many to discover that apart from the early chapters of Genesis, there is no further mention of Eve in the Hebrew Bible until she reappears in the Book of Sirach, written in the second century BCE.[35] The author, Ben Sira, says: "From a woman was the beginning of sin, and because of her we all died" (Sirach 25:24). He states bluntly that sin and death came into the world through woman. Although in the Genesis account, the woman is given the name Eve, which means the mother of the living, Ben Sira, by contrast, makes her the mother of death. He is the first known author to blame woman for sin and death, and has provided one of the most persistent interpretations of the Genesis narrative. Anne Primavesi remarks:

> The connection made by Ben Sira between sin, death and woman has been so accepted into Christian consciousness that it has been assumed that as God did not want her to eat (sin), neither did God want her to die. It was her own fault that she did both.[36]

It was only with Ben Sira that woman becomes identified with sin. The concept of a "fall" does not appear in the Genesis 3 narrative, nor do we find it anywhere in the Hebrew Scriptures. The idea of the "fall" comes from Greek literature, where Plato talks about heavenly perfections shedding their wings and *falling* to earth to be implanted and born as humans. Literal interpretations that treated this myth as history and confused it with an Augustinian interpretation of original sin have done enormous harm to generations of Christians. Eve has been made to bear the sins of the world. As we begin to expose the bias against women in these canonized interpretations, and the inferiorization of women presumed in the exegesis, we will see Eve in a new light. As Eve and, by extension, all other women are given their rightful place, it is to be hoped that the Eve–Mary parallelism will lose its significance.

Traditional Images of Mary Legitimate Women's Oppression

The early patriarchalization of church and ministry was legitimated theologically and christologically. Through the centuries, the resultant image of woman, usually as mother, complementing man as father, became one of submissiveness and dependence. Her images in church and society reinforced one another. As the status of women and the influence of the feminine declined, the cult of Mary grew. Rosemary Haughton explains:

> ...the feminine element in the body of Christ had to find a way to be effective and "present," and did so in the powerful symbol of Mary, whose liturgy acquired some of the Wisdom passages to celebrate her nature and activity.[37]

Searching for an Alternative Tradition

Symbols and doctrines are signposts and guides in our tradition on our long journey to a more complete self-understanding. But without critical interpretation, the Mary symbols will not regain the effective and directive power that many of them had for us. In setting Mary apart from the rest of women, the early writers seemed to suggest that she was acceptable because she did not share the corruption that was inevitably attached to the female condition. While theology searches for an alternative tradition and avails of contemporary exegesis of the creation narratives, the past may serve it with models, but theology must find new meaning in other symbols that are deeply rooted in Christian consciousness.

There is a certain urgency to this search, for the worldwide awakening of the dignity of women in human history is calling for a meaningful presentation of the Mary symbols for contemporary times. This is possible today because women's imagination is beginning to be granted its proper place in theology.

In the past the symbol of Mary modified or at least balanced the exaggerated controlling tendencies in Christian theology that spoke of God in patriarchal as well as imperialistic and triumphalistic metaphors. God existed apart from the world and ruled it externally, either directly through divine intervention or indirectly through controlling the will of human beings. The fact that quasi-divine qualities have been attributed to Mary through the centuries points to a deep intuition that symbolizing God in exclusively dominating images, as father, ruler, lawgiver, and manager of history, is inadequate. Mary cannot be a liberating symbol for women as long as she represents the complementary underside of this "masculine" domination. She becomes emancipating only when she is seen as a radical symbol of a new humanity, freed from hierarchical power relations, either with God or with humanity. She represents "the reconciled wholeness of women and men, nature and humans, creation and God, in the new heaven and the new earth."[38]

Questions for Reflection and Discussion

1. Symbols invite us to participate in their meaning. What are the symbols that evoke and carry religious meaning for you at this time?

2. The dominant Christian culture has been patriarchal. How has this culture influenced marian symbols and prayers? Give some examples.

How has the symbol of Mary modified these patriarchal images?

3. History has not been kind to Eve. Phyllis Trible, in Chapter IV of her book *God and the Rhetoric of Sexuality,* offers a different picture of Eve. Compare Trible's exegesis with that of the traditional interpretation of Genesis 2 and 3 and with that of Ben Sira.

4. Why does placing Mary on a pedestal and contrasting her with sinful Eve reinforce the "Madonna–whore syndrome" that is so destructive of women?

Suggestions for Further Reading

Arbuckle, Gerard A. "Communicating Through Symbols," *Human Development*, Vol 8, No 1, Spring 1987, pp. 7-12.

Børresen, Kari. "Mary in Catholic Theology," *Concilium* 168, eds. Hans Küng and Jürgen Moltmann. Edinburgh: T. T. & Clarke, October 1983.

Johnson, Elizabeth. "The Marian Tradition and the Reality of Women," *Horizons* 12/1 (1985).

McFague, Sallie. *Models of God: Theology for an Ecological, Nuclear Age.* Philadelphia: Fortress Press, 1985.

CHAPTER SEVEN

TOWARD AN ALTERNATIVE
MARIAN THEOLOGY

Mary Has Borne the Image of the Divine

In the preceding chapters we have suggested that one of the primary reasons for the growth of the cult of Mary through history lies in her symbolic power. While official doctrine may have made a distinction between the adoration of God and the veneration of Mary on the intellectual level, the majority of Catholics continue to experience the loving concern of God in the figure of a woman. When speaking of Mary and the feminine, one has to acknowledge the tension between the perspective that considers the feminine evil and seductive, and that which appeals to the feminine for mercy, caring, and forgiveness.

Exaggerations in Medieval Theology

Medieval writers divided the kingdom of God into two zones, justice and mercy; Jesus was the King of Justice, while Mary was always the Queen of Mercy. As an exaggerated emphasis on God's transcendent justice flourished, devotion to Mary progressed proportionately. In this long historical process, the God of Christian belief became ever more remote and judgmental. It was believed that it was impossible for God to forgive sin without demanding satisfaction, so an experience of divine mercy found its expression in Mary. It was she who assumed the life-giving, motherly qualities so characteristic of the God whom Jesus preached about. She thereby helped to balance an inadequate, diminished understanding of God as a benevolent, yet powerful patriarch. In revealing the intimate healing aspects of divine activity, she insured the appreciation of the religious value of bodiliness, sensitivity, and the caring qualities conventionally associated with women.

In the marian tradition, what is often actually being mediated in devotion to the compassionate Mother is a gracious experience of God. Devotion to the Mother of God is often devotion to God the Mother.[1] As compassionate mother, Mary represents ultimate graciousness, unfailing mercy, and is always ready to respond to human need. No wonder her feasts have multiplied and devotion to her is expressed in works of art, in cathedrals built in her honor, and in miracles performed in her name.

During this long historical process, devotion to Mary at first paralleled and then outshone that of the Godhead. Psalms were rewritten in her honor, substituting Mary for God: "Sing to Our Lady a new song, for she hath done wonderful things."[2] She was also prayed to as "Our Mother who art in heaven," who could be depended upon to give us our daily bread. Elizabeth Johnson, commenting on this medieval period, adds that so great was the role of Mary's mercy that theologians ascribed to her what New Testament writers had ascribed to Christ:

> For in her the fullness of the Godhead dwelt corporeally (Col 2:9); of her fullness we have all received (Jn 1:16); because she had emptied herself, God had highly exalted her, so that at her name, every knee would bend.[3]

The figure of Mary had assumed divine prerogatives, prerogatives that properly belong to God.

An Underdeveloped Pneumatology

Theological reflection on the Holy Spirit has traditionally been explored only after first investigating questions on God as Father, God incarnate in Jesus, the relationship of the Father and the Son, and divine creation and redemption. Elizabeth Johnson has observed that theology of the Spirit has remained in an embryonic state.[4] She also adds that the situation was so critical that even Thomas Aquinas had difficulty finding an appropriate name for the Spirit:

While there are two processions in the God, one of these, the procession of love, has no proper name of its own....Hence the relations also which follow from this procession are without a name: for
which reason the person proceeding in that manner has not a proper name.[5]

In recent times and especially since Vatican II, Catholic theologians
have paid great attention to the criticism coming especially from
Protestant scholars that Catholics have substituted devotion to Mary for
an experience of the Holy Spirit. In a much-quoted article, "Mary and the
Protestant Mind," Elsie Gibbon observes:

When I began to study Catholic theology, every place I expected to
find an exposition of the doctrine of the Holy Spirit, I found Mary.
What Protestants universally attribute to the action of the Holy
Spirit was attributed to Mary.[6]

Devotion to Mary has occupied spaces left vacant by an underdeveloped pneumatology or a theology of the Holy Spirit. (*Pneuma* is the Greek
word for Spirit.) Catholics frequently give the impression that Mary is
spiritually present to guide and inspire, that she forms Christ in believers
and is their link with him, and that it is through her that believers go to
Jesus. She has been called mediatrix, intercessor, advocate, helper, con-
soler—titles that belong to the Holy Spirit, the Counselor: "And I will ask
the Father, and he will give you another Counselor, to be with you for
ever" (John 14:16). In the Scriptures the Holy Spirit is the enabling power
of salvation who has always been associated with divine intimacy and
presence to people's lives.

In a contemporary theology of the Trinity the qualities of sanctifying,
interceding, and consoling, borne by the figure of Mary, will have to be
retrieved again for the Holy Spirit, whose reality and activity have virtu-
ally been lost from much of Christian theological consciousness. Then
God can be imaged as mystery, closer to us than we are to ourselves, and
the reality of the divine presence can once more be experienced as intimate and energizing. God is not self-contained and self-absorbed. God, a
mystery beyond all imagining, is overflowing love, unfathomably merciful with an outreaching desire for union with all that God has made. This

communion of divine life is with us in Christ and as Spirit. "God's love has been poured into our hearts through the Holy Spirit that has been given to us" (Romans 5:5) and who is breathed forth upon us, empowering us to be born and reborn in the midst of the oppressive structures of our world.

The word "Spirit," like all other words used for God, is an analogy. In the Scriptures it is associated with breathing, burning fire, wind, and light. These images evoke and emphasize "the mobile, outgoing, living essence of love, the very antithesis of stasis."[7] It is not Mary but the Holy Spirit who is the source of life. It is not Mary but the Holy Spirit who is the indwelling of the divine mystery and who continues to renew the face of the earth. Mary's place in salvation history is rather to bear witness to the presence of this divine mystery in the church.

Some attempts in recent years to explain the Trinity have spoken about the Spirit as the feminine person of the godhead,[8] with the feminine Spirit restricted to bearing the presence of God to the world. Considering the Holy Spirit as the feminine side of God leads to further difficulties, leaving us with two masculine images and a nebulous third person—"two men and a bird," as the facetious title of a recent article on the Trinity expressed it. Speaking about the feminine dimension of God does not help us to appreciate that female imagery by itself can point to God and has the capacity to represent God.

Speaking of God in Finite Images

Images of God aim at evoking an experience of the divine. The mystery of God, a living mystery of relationships, transcends all finite images, for no one image can capture or exhaustively express the holy mystery. In the Christian tradition God has been spoken of as King of Kings, Lord of Lords, monarch, and ruler to whom we owe unquestioning obedience, conveying the idea that God is both similar to and represented by patriarchal leadership. It is the world of men that has provided the paradigm for the symbol of God as man and ruler within a patriarchal system. The problem lies not in the fact that male metaphors are used, but that they are used *exclusively* and *literally*. For instance, because God as father has become an overliteralized metaphor, the symbol of God as mother is eclipsed.

Feminist theological discourse emphasizes that using exclusively male images excludes female reality as suitable metaphor for God, which in turn denigrates the dignity of women and justifies the dominance of men in society. Such exclusive use of male images also makes female images seem to lose their religious significance and ability to point to ultimate truth.

Images of God as female are necessary for a fuller expression of God as mystery. Because these have been suppressed in official formulations and teaching, they came to be embodied in the figure of Mary, who functioned to reveal the unfailing love of God that obtains grace for sinners.

In a tradition where women have not been taken seriously as dialogue partners, and where nearness to God has often meant distance from women, Mary can represent the image of woman in her relationship to God, equally capable of imaging the divine.

Imaging God in Male and Female Metaphors

Male and female metaphors evoke different images of God. Each brings its own sense of God, and each is needed to represent God, not only as nurturing and caring, but also as powerful, initiating, creating, and redeeming. Since the feminine has been excluded from participating in God, divine imagery has become impoverished.

Speaking of God in female metaphors does not mean that God has a feminine dimension any more than speaking of God in male metaphors means that God has a masculine dimension. God does not have "dimensions."[9] If women are created in the image of God, then female metaphors can speak of God in as full and as limited a way as male metaphors. Female imagery has the capacity to represent God not only as compassionate, but also as challenging the powers of the world through the vitalizing grace of the Spirit. Johnson offers a provocative insight:

> Since it is women whose bodies bear, nourish, and deliver new persons into life and, as society is traditionally structured, are most often charged with the responsibility to nurture and raise them into maturity, language about God as mother carries a unique power to express human relationship to the mystery who generates and cares for everything.[10]

Today more than ever the Christian message needs to emphasize God's compassion and mercy. Our world needs the gifts of our intuition and graciousness, our questioning intellect, our capacity for righteous anger, as well as our profound capacity for understanding and love. These are attributes for all Christians, not just for women. Once we can envision God's mystery as caring and immanent, as well as just and transcendent, the figure of Mary will not have to function to bring a distant patriarchal God close to us, for God is always present in, and to, creation. It is in God that we live and move and have our being (Acts 17:28). Nor will Mary's role consist of bearing the imagery of the divine in the Christian tradition.

The only option for Christian theology, as Catherine LaCugna shows, is a trinitarian one, that is, one that starts from its original basis in the experience of being saved by God in Christ in the power of the Holy Spirit. At present the Trinity, as it is understood, has little connection with people's life experience, and its doctrine is too complicated to understand. It is *in* Christ that we meet the living God whom Jesus proclaimed, and it is *through* Christ that we remain faithful to the living God. Such a theology, says LaCugna, will explore "the mysteries of love, relationship, personhood and communion within the framework of God's self revelation in the person of Christ and the activity of the Holy Spirit."[11]

It is the essence of God to be in relationship to other persons. This is a mystery of self-giving and self-receiving; there is no room for inequality, division, or hierarchy. We therefore need new ways of imaging God as triune, images that will symbolize God's radical self-giving in incarnation and grace.

Reflection on the biblical God of compassion, our participation in the life of God through Jesus, and the return of pneumatology to theological discussion all bring new opportunities for thinking about God not as a remote and transcendent being who miraculously intervenes in our lives, but as an all-encompassing source of divine love and life. The practical import of this reflection, says LaCugna, is that "entering into the life of God means entering into the deepest way possible into the economy, into the life of Jesus Christ, into the life of the Spirit, into the life of others."[12]

Such contemplation will free us to focus on Mary in her proper context as a creature of God, totally sanctified and overshadowed by the Holy Spirit. But first of all this reflection will entail emptying ourselves of preconceived notions about God and Mary and "ridding ourselves of images, symbols and ideas that stand in the way of experiencing the living God."[13] The ways in which we address God offer us an indication of how we view

God; they also reveal a lot about how we view ourselves. Because language shapes worlds of meaning for us, it requires ongoing revision. Religious language too needs revisioning if we are not to impoverish and falsify how we name and address God.

Theology's Ideological Bias

We have inherited a classical theology that has not been aware of its own ideological bias—created by and supportive of a patriarchal society. Mariologists were either clerics or monks who held power within the church, and were, therefore, socially marginalized. As captives of the viewpoint of their culture, and reflecting the religious interests of their particular social class, they envisioned the image of God, and of Mary, as that of the power-holding, ruling class. It is understandable, therefore, that marian thought and symbols would have been shaped by androcentric perspectives.

Second, certain themes just could not make their way into the conscious horizon of traditional theology and of marian theology in particular. During the last twenty years, Christian feminist theologians have challenged the androcentric, hierarchical character of the western religious tradition. They have insisted that the humanity of women be given equal status and that theology analyze the dualistic divisions that separate people, male/female, soul/body, reason/ emotion, spiritual/material. Avoiding such dualisms encourages the recognition and appreciation of human personality characteristics common to both men and women. It also helps to focus the discussion on the community rather than on gender-assigned characteristics.

In an insightful comment, Karl Rahner reminds us that it was the image of woman that enabled the church in past centuries to prevent society, with which it was often too uncritically identified, from setting up a purely male domination. He adds that the church had to learn slowly and painfully amid the changes in secular society:

to give woman what is due to her by nature and by right: an historical process which is still far from complete. But in its understanding of faith the Church has a starting point of its own and a dynamism of its own for this process. And what is its own is in fact present as an archetype in its image of Mary.[14]

Spirituality today must develop, not against the body, but in and through the body, and through relationships with one another. In a world where models of domination, global warfare and militarism, and starvation and poverty seem to dominate, Christian feminists are claiming Mary as a critical symbol of compassionate love amid the struggles of history. When she is free of the burden of keeping alive the female imagery of the divine, she can then be retrieved as a genuine woman and disciple, concerned for and offering hope to the marginalized and oppressed of our world (Luke 1:52–53).

Mary, a Finite Human Being with a Unique Role in History

Statements about Mary ought to focus on her as a historical and finite human being who has a definite though unique place in history. The church will always see her as the one who had an exceptional function in salvation history. Rahner, however, cautions that her exceptional function in history does not allow us "to ascribe to her alone the whole fullness of human reality, which can be realized only in humankind as a whole and in the whole of history."[15] She must be envisioned as a poor woman who lived in the context of the sociohistorical and religious situation of her time. Rahner adds that we must focus on Mary:

> not as a heavenly being, but as a human person, as active and suffering for herself and others, as learning in the midst of many uncertainties, as accepting her function in salvation history in faith, hope, and love, and by this very fact, as model and mother of believers.[16]

Political and Liberation Theologies

As theology retrieves for the mystery of God those elements in the marian symbol that properly belong to the Godhead, mariology is being purified from pious exaggerations. In a corresponding development, the person of Mary is once again becoming important in the liberation theologies of oppressed peoples. These theologies are concerned with the redefinition of power and ultimately the redefinition of society. They have arisen from the experience of oppressed groups who find in Mary a symbol of hope in their struggle toward liberation. Leonardo and Clodovis Boff describe her as:

...Mary from Nazareth, a woman of the people, who observed popular religious customs of the time...who worried about her son...and who followed him to the foot of the cross....Because of this ordinariness, and not in spite of it, Mary is everything that faith proclaims her to be....[17]

Johannes Metz[18] suggests that political theologians use the categories of memory, narrative, and solidarity to provide an intellectual base for the construction of their theologies. The act of remembering our solidarity with our leaders and saints who have gone before us, and narrating stories about their efforts and struggles to bring about liberation, have the power to inspire us to action on behalf of justice. The saints who have gone before us are heralds of God's grace in the midst of conflict. It is in this context that Mary has captured the imagination of the poor. They contemplate her as a prophet of God for the poor of her day, singing in anticipation her song of liberation, and realizing God's plan of liberation in history.

Leonardo Boff[19] stresses that Mary in particular is a herald of liberation, singing the song of justice of the coming kingdom of God (Luke 1:46–55). The poor and the marginalized of our world can rediscover her solidarity with them. This may be a good starting point for a theological reflection on Mary, the mother of Jesus, who was his disciple and a woman of faith. It is the task of liberation theologians, he says, to develop a prophetic image of Mary:

...as the strong, determined woman, the woman committed to the messianic liberation of the poor from the historical social injustices under which they suffer. And today we see this image taking shape, deep in the heart of an oppressed people, who long for a voice in society and liberation from its evils.[20]

The poor can identify with a poor village woman, a member of a people oppressed by foreign rulers; they understand what it means to be a refugee fleeing with her newborn child, or bereaving the untimely death of her son, a victim of unjust execution.

The Latin American bishops believe that female symbolism can be rescued in a way that can promote the full humanity of women. As the Third General Conference of the Latin American Bishops states:

in Mary, the Gospel has penetrated femininity, redeeming it and exalting it....Mary guarantees the greatness of the feminine, indicating the specific way of being woman with her vocation to be the soul, the gift, capable of spiritualizing the flesh and embodying the Spirit.[21]

Feminist Theology

Like liberation theology, feminist theology takes its starting point from the experience of the oppressed. The feminist perspective is an orientation to theology as a whole and has as its critical principle the promotion of the full humanity of women, up to now marginalized in theory as well as in reality. It cautions, however, that to stress that women need emancipation implies that men are already freed.[22] It therefore denounces whatever is dehumanizing to women *and* men and announces the transformation of society. Feminist theologians are already finding cracks in the long Christian tradition, a tradition where division and difference have often been given more emphasis than similarity and relationships. They are also examining a traditional spirituality that developed at a terrible price as regards the natural affections of men and women and the natural humanity of women. The search has already begun for an alternative tradition.

While liberation theologians are concerned with a redefinition of power and society, feminist theologians are especially concerned with a redefinition of relationships. It is not enough to reflect on society as it is at present but on how it ought to be. Since individuals create and are created by the society in which they live, conversion of the individual *and* of the oppressive structures of society are needed to create a new culture, a new nature, a new way of being in the world. Therefore, the distorted symbol systems that support these structures need changing so that a new community characterized by mutuality and freedom becomes possible in church and society. Finally, these theologians note that in any society the poorest of the poor are women, especially those who struggle alone to care for and raise children, or who are abused or marginalized. They, in a very special way, cry out for compassion.

Karl Rahner believes that if marian theology wants to present an image of Mary that is meaningful for our times, that image "can perhaps be produced authentically today only by women, by women theologians,"[23] and Hans Urs von Balthasar (who himself was opposed to the ordination of women) complains about the imbalance of the male principle in the church so that:

> it has to a large extent put off its mystical characteristics; it has become a church of permanent conversations, organizations, advisory commissions, congresses, synods...structures and restructurings, sociological experiments, statistics, that is to say, more than ever a male church, if perhaps one should not say a sexless entity.[24]

And again, in his fear that Christianity threatens imperceptibly to become inhuman, he adds:

> ...in this masculine world, all that we have is one ideology replacing another, everything becomes polemical, critical, bitter, humorless, and ultimately boring, and people in their masses run away from the church.[25]

A feminist theology of Mary is taking on a completely new form and is offering a very different image of her from the traditional, culturally conditioned images that do little to uplift women in search of a full humanity. Precisely as a woman her story will undoubtedly resonate with those of other women through bonds of sisterhood. The self-possessed poor woman of the annunciation narrative (Luke 1:28–33) who finds favor with God and is willing to cooperate with God's plan of salvation is a model of courage for the marginalized women of today's world. She stands in solidarity with the poorest of the poor of society. Elizabeth Johnson adds that "this solidarity carries political significance, for it is to *this* kind of woman that God has done great things."[26]

The challenge offered to us by these praxis-oriented theologies suggests that we take the liberation stance as a hermeneutic with which to reread the significance of Mary for our times. The historic figure of Mary now enters into dialogue with contemporary times, cultures, and problems, and with the people who work to make the values of the kingdom of God an actuality in our world. Our starting point of necessity is the experience of the oppressed and marginalized of society.

Retrieving the Figure of Mary

Bernard Lonergan draws our attention to a highly significant change in the contemporary understanding of theology. While theology used to be defined as a science about God "with one system valid for all times and places,"[27] its task today is to explain faith in God at each point in history and in different cultural contexts. In this understanding theologians must critique the silent and submissive images that have presented Mary as sweet and uncomplaining and that do little to uplift marginalized and oppressed women "the battered, the tortured, the hungry, the silenced and the unfree."[28] Mary must be retrieved as a woman strong and resourceful, our sister in faith who did not hesitate to proclaim God's concern for the oppressed.

Retrieving the historical figure of Mary must be done in the context of the complexity of the contemporary world. This is a world characterized by militarization, domination, and the coercion of the weak by the strong. The stockpiling of nuclear arms and the irreversible destruction of our planet Earth suggest the seriousness and diversity of the problem. The violence and grinding poverty, the brutality of political repression, and the destitution of the many call for our compassion.

This is also, however, a world that is beginning to resist dualism, polarization, and the politics of domination/submission. Ecological awareness and an appreciation of an inclusive, nonhierarchical vision of reality are two current themes that have emerged in world consciousness and that will have profound implications for the world and the church into the next century. Movements that are profoundly creative and caring are bringing the riches of their insight into the life-giving systems of world and church, and are challenging relationships and structures. It is in the context of this new world consciousness of the appreciation of the caring qualities, traditionally associated with the feminine, that we look to Mary as our model.

Mary, Our Model Disciple

Mary's commitment to God's plan for her at the annunciation and her identifying herself with Jesus' mission establish her as the central figure representing the kingdom of God. These choices include a desire to change the sinful social realities of her time. Biblical and theological scholarship, as well as recent magisterial documents, highlight her as a model of active discipleship:

She is held up as an example for the way in which, in her own particular life, she fully and responsibly accepted God's will (see Luke 1:38), because she heard the Word of God and acted on it, and because charity and a spirit of service are the driving force of her actions. She is worthy of imitation because she was the first and most perfect of Christ's disciples.[29]

While Jesus' ministry is open to all, it is directed primarily to those excluded and ignored by the social and religious systems of his time. The poor are always the insignificant, the anonymous, the "nonpersons" of history. Their identification with Mary, the mother of Jesus, who shared their human story and who was chosen to play an important role in God's liberating action in history, can lend dignity to the lives of those devalued by society. This identification locates Mary firmly among us as our model Christian disciple. She calls us to give voice to the pain of those who cannot articulate either the protest or the hope of her own Magnificat. There is no room for timidity here, for, like Mary, we too are called to hear the word of God and keep it.

Contemporary theological reflection on Mary is focusing on the disciple of Jesus who was also his mother. Her personal involvement in the birth of the Messiah, as well as her own lifelong faith in God, has intimately linked her with the mystery of the world's salvation. Any liturgical or devotional presentation of Mary must clearly call the church to the inclusive, liberating, and prophetic discipleship that Mary embodies. As Gustavo Gutiérrez reminds us, "Her contemplation of God's holiness is not an evasion of history; her joy at the gratuitous love of the Lord does not make her forget the demands of justice."[30] The liberating song of Mary (Luke 1:46–55), in the liberating tradition of Miriam, Deborah, Hannah, and Judith, points to the new order of creation that is good news to the poor and the marginalized of society.

Questions for Reflection and Discussion

1. In medieval theology the figure of Mary assumed divine prerogatives. What particular images of God provoked this development?

2. Because theological reflection on the Holy Spirit has been largely neglected in the Christian tradition, Mary has assumed functions that biblically belong to the paraclete (John 14:16; 15:26; 16:7). What are these

functions? Give examples of how Christian piety has attributed them to Mary.

3. The problem of speech about God lies not in the fact that male metaphors are used, but that they are used literally and often exclusively. How have these images been detrimental to an appreciation of the mystery of God? How have they been harmful to the interpretation of the nature of women?

4. Liberation theologians today are asking us to claim Mary as a model Christian disciple. What is the scriptural basis and starting point for such a claim? How might contemporary marian devotions that have yet to be purified of pious exaggerations be a hindrance?

Suggestions for Further Reading

Bingemer, Maria Clara. "Woman: Time and Eternity, the Eternal Woman and the Feminine Face of God," *Concilium* 194, eds. Anne Carr and Elisabeth Fiorenza, 1991/6.

Halkes, Catharina. "Mary and Women," *Concilium* 168, eds. Hans Küng and Jürgen Moltmann, October 1983.

Johnson, Elizabeth. "Mary and the Image of God," and "Reconstructing a Theology of Mary," *Mary, Woman of Nazareth,* ed. Doris Donnelly. New York: Paulist Press, 1989.

———. *She Who Is: The Mystery of God in Feminist Theological Discourse.* New York: Crossroad, 1994, pp. 124-149.

LaCugna, Catherine. "God in Communion With Us," *Freeing Theology: The Essentials of Theology in Feminist Perspective,* ed. Catherine LaCugna. San Francisco: HarperSanFrancisco, 1993, pp. 83-114.

MARY IN POPULAR BELIEF

Popular Religion

The faithful have constantly venerated Mary and turned to her in time of need to seek her help and mercy. Throughout the history of the church, certain Christians have claimed that the mother of Jesus has manifested herself to them. From the Middle Ages onwards, as devotion to the Blessed Virgin became an ever more integral part of Catholic devotional life, claims of marian apparitions or manifestations have become more widespread. Four of the most famous and universally recognized apparitions are the appearances of Our Lady of Guadalupe, Our Lady of Lourdes, Our Lady of La Salette, and Our Lady of Fatima.

In the Philippines, the veneration of Mary has taken the form of visiting marian shrines, particularly those of Antipolo, Manaog, and Baclaran. In Pakistan, the national marian shrine at Miriamabad draws large numbers of pilgrims annually. Our discussion on Mary in the Christian tradition would not be complete, therefore, without a general comment on popular religion and the phenomena of pilgrimage and apparitions.

Popular religion is intensely human and emotionally charged, yet tends to be uncritical in accepting propositions of faith. It often seeks tangible proof, like physical signs and wonders, as a sign of the presence of the divine. Pilgrim shrines and the miracles that happen there affirm the presence of the divine. The relationship between the believer and God, or the believer and Mary, is often a contractual one. In return for prayer, penance, or the fulfillment of a vow, God bestows favors. Because of the growing enthusiasm for marian apparitions and visions and the constant stream of pilgrims to marian shrines, we will first examine the important role of pilgrimage in the Christian tradition.

Pilgrimage in the Christian Tradition

Sites of pilgrimage are believed to be places where miracles once happened or may happen again. They represent a "tear in the veil" that separates heaven from earth.[1] In Christendom, monastic contemplatives and mystics were concerned about daily interior salvific journeys. For the laity, pilgrimage was the great liminal experience of the religious life. Victor and Edith Turner state it succinctly: "If mysticism is an interior pilgrimage, pilgrimage is exteriorized mysticism."[2] One purifies oneself by penance and travel. The pilgrim visits a holy site or holy shrine. In most pilgrimages magical beliefs abound: beliefs in relics, images, and the efficacy of water from sacred springs, but these only benefit the pilgrim who has had a conversion of heart. When a pilgrimage system becomes established, it operates like other social institutions. Liturgies and devotional services at the sites of pilgrimage are structured, and sometimes seasons of pilgrimage are established to cater to the large number of pilgrims. Ideally, however, pilgrimage is charismatic. It is a pilgrim's decision or personal response to a charism. Therefore orthodox religion tends to be ambivalent toward it.

While there is a vast body of literature about marian apparitions, most of it is devotional or apologetic. Its authors are interested in defending and publicizing what they believe to be appearances of the Virgin Mary. Scholarly writings about apparitions are scarce.[3] This makes it difficult for those who wish to study the nature of apparitions and related phenomena, the sociohistorical and religious contexts in which they occur, the worldview of the devotees, and their relationship to Mary (or the saints). Such studies must explore the meaning of apparitions for the visionaries themselves and the process by which they draw meaning from the apparition experiences.

Marian Apparitions and Church Teaching

There is no definitive church teaching about what happens during an apparition. Some theologians suggest that an apparition is a manifestation of the charismatic element of the church in which a person's imagination is inspired to receive a message from heaven. Others suggest that such an occurrence could be interpreted as the nearness of God to those who are outside the official channels of access to the holy.

Although theologians may interpret the phenomenon in various ways, they accept that visions or apparitions, considered private revelations by the church's magisterium, cannot add to or embellish the deposit of faith. If genuine, they can only enhance devotion to, and perhaps the understanding of, faith. As with other devotional practices, however, official church approval does not mean that the faithful are required to believe in apparitions or in their historicity. They are to be respected in so far as they inspire people to deeper faith and consistent social action, and they are to be judged by their fruits: love, justice, and peace. Here is a word of caution from the U.S. Catholic bishops:

> Even when a private revelation has spread to the entire world, as in the case of Our Lady of Lourdes, and has been recognized in the liturgical calendar, the Church does not make mandatory the acceptance either of the original story or of particular forms of piety springing from it.[4]

Expressing the Experience of the Holy

We know from our religious behavior that the human psyche reaches for concrete symbols when it tries to express its experience of the holy. In Israel it was the ark and the temple; in Christianity it is the church, the sacraments, and sacramentals. The temple and the church are holy ground, sacred space, where one experiences the divine in a special way. In the marian apparitions, the visionary experiences something marvelous that was never before experienced. It is as if she or he is prepared to accept a great theophany, in this case the manifestation of the Mother of God. The apparitions are usually experienced by the poor, mostly poor women, and the young, and the theophanies are described in great detail. Gebara and Bingemer explain that something extraordinary happens on the level of human relationships. When normal words and gestures are no longer convincing, the "divine" moves in to say what the human heart already knows but is not heeding.

> ...[the] theophany is the great poetry of human beings; it is the most

advanced use of symbols and sometimes of the prophetic ability to denounce existing evil and to demand that justice be restored.[5]

Therefore in the apparitions,

...a constant is the "extraordinary" element that breaks up the ordinariness of life and interferes with the normal functioning of nature. It is as though the theophany or appearance sought to indicate the need to change something radically.[6]

Certain Constants in the Marian Apparitions

There are certain constants in the image of Mary as she is experienced by visionaries through the centuries. The first popular image of Mary has been that of healer and restorer of health. In the Middle Ages, when medical knowledge was more limited and causes of many illnesses were unknown, people sought divine healing. Mary's many shrines became places for seeking cures, and numerous miraculous healings have been attributed to her. Whether these cures came from natural or psychological means made no difference. They were accepted as miraculous by those who were relieved from their suffering. While modern advancement in medicine influences our assessment of contemporary healing, the claim of miraculous cures at marian shrines still persists, especially at Lourdes, for people continue to seek miracles when science fails to provide a cure.

Another constant in popular religious imagination is that Mary remains an intercessor between heaven and earth. Not only does she plead with God on our behalf but because she is God's mother, she actually influences God's judgments. As Mother of Mercy, she uses her intercessory powers especially to intervene on our behalf and ensure our salvation. Belief in her power to plead to God on our behalf has added to the power and popularity of her shrines and the stories of miracles attached to them. In this century, not only does she intercede for sinners but she has become an outspoken critic of communism. At Fatima, for example, she called for prayers for the conversion of Russia.

The Symbol of Guadalupe

Our Lady of Guadalupe, originally the patroness of Mexico, has become more and more acknowledged as the Mother of the Americas.[7] Devotion to her stands at the very origins of Mexican Christianity. Tepeyac, the location of Mary's apparition, had been the sacred site of Tonantzin, the Indian mother goddess, from very ancient times. Tepeyac, some five miles north of Mexico City, was the site of pilgrimages for centuries, and people had come from far and near to worship the mother goddess. Our Lady appeared there on December 9, 1531, to an Aztec Indian whose indigenous name was Single Eagle but whose Christian name was Juan Diego. She identified herself with Tonantzin, the goddess of the subjugated people, not only in her body, language, and clothing, but also in her choice of ancient Indian holy place and in the celestial symbols surrounding her. The flowers and the music of the vision were also part of the goddess' temple worship.

It was at this site that Mary spoke to the people with tenderness, requested their cooperation, and asked them to become her missionaries. She identified herself as the "ever virgin, Mary, Mother of the true God who gives life and maintains it in existence."[8]

This message of hope came at a time when the Mexican nation was being exploited by the *conquistadores*, the representatives of the Spanish crown who had come to conquer Mexico. The enslavement of the native peoples whose very humanity was being debated, the raping and degradation of their women, and the efforts to totally eradicate their religion, brought the nation to the verge of despair. The crushed dignity of the people was restored in the person of Juan Diego, and through him they were called upon to be Mary's trusted messengers. Juan Diego had no difficulty understanding her, for she spoke in his native language. Speaking to him with dignity and respect, she challenged the people to rise above their situation of marginalization and oppression and to assume responsibility for their life and future. In Mary, too, Mexican womanhood, which had been prostituted against by the conquistadors, was once more restored to its original dignity.[9]

In asking Juan Diego to go to the bishop, Mary supported the authority of the church's ministers and upheld the meaning of the church as communion. In asking the poor to become her messengers she was inviting the Spanish missionaries to commit themselves to them and to move out to the periphery and serve them. This was at the same time an invitation to appreciate the value of their indigenous culture and to assimilate them into the community of the church. The symbol of Mary at Guadalupe is therefore a powerful symbol for the people of Mexico, for it assimilates an ancient religious figure into her Mexican representation. She appears carrying the Christ Child in her womb, offering the people new life and hope in the person of her Son, who is coming to be incarnated in their lives and culture.

Elizabeth Johnson says that the figure of Our Lady of Guadalupe:

> combined the Indian female expression of God, which the Spanish had tried to wipe out as diabolical, with the Spanish male expression of God which the Indians had found incomprehensible (for everything which is perfect in the Nahuatl cosmovision has a male and female component). Each understanding of God was expanded by the other, yielding a new mestizo expression which enriches the very understanding of the selfhood of God.[10]

The cult of Our Lady of Guadalupe mediates the compassionate reality of God in the form of a woman. Her all-encompassing warmth and love convey a strength of presence as well as care for the little ones. She has been an inspiration to the people in their continuing struggle toward the full realization of political and economic independence and indigenous religious expression. While the struggle for justice continues, this powerful symbol continues to be associated with the social and political liberation of the people, not only in Mexico but throughout the Americas. It is fitting, therefore, that she has been proclaimed patron saint of all the Americas.

Marian Pilgrimages in the Nineteenth and Twentieth Centuries

Marian pilgrimages and images had a dramatic resurgence in the nineteenth and early twentieth centuries. In less than fifty years, from 1928-1971, a total of 210 apparitions can be cited.[11] Whereas medieval pilgrimages began as local or regional devotions to Mary, postindustrial-age pilgrimages owe their origin to particular visionary or apparitional experiences. The first among them was the so-called Miraculous Medal of Catherine Labouré (1806-76). The medal's design included the image of the Virgin within an oval frame with the words "O Mary, conceived without sin, pray for us who have recourse to thee." It was soon distributed all over the world in millions, and its tremendous popularity and the miracles attributed to it helped to impress the doctrine of the immaculate conception on the consciousness of Catholic people. This in turn led to a growing demand to have the doctrine solemnly defined.

The Apparitions at Lourdes

The apparitions of the Blessed Virgin to Bernadette Soubirous at Lourdes on February 11, 1858, led to the establishment of a marian shrine that has become the modern center of marian devotion throughout Christendom. When asked during the church interrogation to describe the Virgin Mary as she saw her, Bernadette replied, "The Blessed Virgin of the parish church for the face and the clothes...but alive and surrounded by light."[12] The story of a poor peasant girl who suffered from asthma all her life and to whom Mary appeared, has gripped the imagination of the whole Catholic world. One of the enduring effects of the story of Lourdes is an increased commitment to belief in the dogma of Mary's immaculate conception, proclaimed as official teaching just four years before the apparitions began. It is also claimed that increasing numbers of pilgrims who pray at the shrine experience repentance and reconciliation, and that crippled bodies are healed.

The Apparitions at La Salette

Some twelve years earlier in a similarly out-of-the-way place, at La Salette, France, two young children herding cattle came home and reported that they had seen a beautiful lady. She was seated and weeping and encircled by a brilliant light. The apparition at La Salette admonished the children to say their prayers faithfully and outlined the punishments the people would suffer because of their sins: harvests would fail and they would only have enough potatoes until Christmas. The lady is reported to have said that she had given them six days to work, reserving the seventh for herself, words that identify her with God. She is also reported to have given each of them a secret, which they were not to divulge to anyone. The two children were repeatedly interrogated to test their stories. According to reports they never introduced the slightest variation into their account.

There are theological difficulties with the visionaries' image of Mary restraining her Son from punishing his people. Since there are no critical accounts based on firsthand sources, as in the case of Lourdes, Hilda Graef adds:

...there seems to be nothing either in the description of the apparition or in its discourses that points unmistakably to a supernatural origin. The so-called "secrets" too, which have been solemnly forbidden to be published by the Church authorities, seem to have contained nothing more than vague apocalyptic threats.[13]

The Apparitions at Fatima

In 1917 the experience at Fatima in Portugal of three young children, Lucia dos Santos and her cousins Francisco and Jacinta Marto, caught the attention of a world at war. The Fatima story began when a young man who identified himself as the angel of peace taught the children to pray. They followed his instructions, praying intensely for a year, and then, in May 1917, a woman dressed in white appeared to them near the Cova de Iria where they tended their flock. She asked them to return on the thirteenth day of every month until October. The children continued to go to the Cova on the prescribed day each month, during which time they were granted apocalyptic visions and prophetic warnings. On October 13, 1917, the woman identified herself as Our Lady of the Rosary. She requested that Russia be consecrated to her immaculate heart and that a communion of reparation be made on the first Saturday of every month. At this last apparition, when the children were granted ecstatic visions, the assembled crowd experienced what has come to be known as the "Miracle of the Sun."

After the Fatima apparitions were authenticated in 1930 interest in them soon increased, especially with the coming of the second world war and the rising power of the Soviet Union. Rumors about the Fatima secrets and especially about the famous third secret, the one that has been revealed only to the popes, still abound.

The Apparitions at Medjugorje

The apparitions that have recently claimed worldwide attention are in Medjugorje, in the former Yugoslavia, starting in 1981. The site where six children have reportedly had visions of the Blessed Virgin Mary has drawn pilgrims and gained devotees from around the world despite the refusal of church authorities to authenticate the appearances. Like the earlier twentieth-century apparitions, Medjugorje too involves prophecies, secrets, and admonitions to prayer and penance.

The Church Calls for Discernment and Prudence

The person who goes on pilgrimage to a marian shrine may have a deep faith experience and return home with a sense of conversion and renewed commitment. However much approved by the church, these apparitions do not belong to what is called the "deposit of faith"; hence we will give them the same merely human credence that we give to any other statement we hold to be true. In private revelations the personality of the recipient plays an important role and can influence even the most authentic experience.

The prerogative of investigating an apparition and of deciding whether it is worthy of "the assent of human faith" belongs officially to the bishop in whose diocese it has occurred. The church realizes only too well that vestiges of magic can be found not only in adults today but also in the doctrines and rituals of advanced religions. It therefore advises discernment and prudence.

Even if an apparition has the approval of the church, we are not obliged to give it our consent if, upon mature reflection, we feel unable to believe in it. Edward Schillebeeckx points out that the church's approval of an apparition or a private revelation is never an infallible proof of its historical truth and authenticity.[14] It means that the church does not regard belief in the apparition to be misguided or harmful to the faithful. It also confirms, as Schillebeeckx emphasizes, that:

> It is merely an official confirmation of the fact that sufficient evidence has emerged from the investigation to enable us to be cautiously certain in our acceptance of the divine authenticity of the apparition on rational grounds...the Church does no more than give her official permission that Mary may be venerated in a special way at the place where the apparition occurred....All that the Church declares is that, in her judgment, they are in no way contrary to faith and morals and that there are sufficient indications for their pious and cautious approval by human faith.[15]

Anne Carr notes that while this upsurge of apparitions in the nineteenth and twentieth centuries aroused great hopes and fears, and their sites attracted pilgrims from all walks of life, these apparitions helped to divinize Mary, while never stressing her active cooperation in Christ's redemption.[16] The apparitions of Lourdes, for example, simply reinforce traditional doctrines. While Gebara and Bingemer's[17] reflections on Mary's appearance at Guadalupe in the sixteenth century focus on the prophetic ability of the theophany to denounce evil and demand justice, Barbara Pope notes that the more recent nineteenth- and twentieth-century apparitions never carried a message of social transformation or the overcoming of exploitation and oppression. Their political direction, she argues, was always backward rather than forward.[18]

The Recent Upsurge of Marian Manifestations

However we may interpret the present phenomenon of marian manifestations and apparitions and the stream of pilgrims to marian shrines, theologians ought to investigate the reasons why the Christian community is drawn to express its faith and devotion, both in belief in the apparitions of the Virgin and in these pilgrimages. Many of the marian apparitions have occurred or continue to occur in countries of dire poverty or where the socioeconomic situation has been very bad. Mary's presence has been a sign of hope that has offered comfort to people's lives. Turner suggests that the recent trend may be a sign of:

> a resurgent "female" principle, after centuries of "male" iconoclasm, technical progress, bureaucratization, the conquest by reason and force of all natural vehicles. May we not retrace the history of Marian pilgrimage, woman's progress from almost anonymous and faceless nurturant vehiclehood to an individuated, liberated femaleness, seen through the "masculine" eyes of Western culture as both nemesis and the coming of a new age?[19]

The Popular Apocalyptic Ideology of Apparitions

A discussion on modern apparitions calls for an examination of the worldview of the participants in these apparitions. For many of them, Mary is the woman "clothed with the sun" (Revelation 12) appearing in very troubled times. She appears pleading, threatening, weeping, and her messages and secrets are related to the contemporary world situation. Representing divine mercy, she intercedes with God or Christ and intervenes in history to change an otherwise predetermined course of events. Her apocalyptic warnings speak of chastisement for the sins of the world. God is portrayed as angry because humanity's sins have disrupted the established order and therefore his justice demands immediate chastisement, a chastisement that can be lessened by prayer and penance. At Medjugorje, for example, Mary told the young visionaries that war would be averted by fasting and prayer, and she stressed that people could be reconciled to God if they prayed, fasted, and went to confession.

The emphasis in the Fatima apparitions on Mary's secrets evokes curiosity and provokes inquiry about the apocalyptic nature of such apparitions. The warnings of Fatima continue in the apparitions to the visionaries at Medjugorje, where the evil of the world is blamed on Satan. John Shinners believes that such messages have as much to do with the visionaries' own perception of their world as they have to do with any special revelation. He sees millennial prophecies as

> ...reproofs against the existing social order. That order has either swept away or radically ordered cherished institutions and customs, or is corrupt and oppressive and therefore must be replaced by a just society, a utopia. Modern marian apparitions consistently see existing society as corrupted by change. They wax nostalgic for the stability, comfort, and predictability of tradition, especially Catholic tradition.[20]

In spite of the apocalyptic warnings and the predictions of the demise of the world, Mary has remained intensely human, blending together the roles of mother and nurturer, comforter and counselor. It is her tender, forgiving, and consoling characteristics that make her so easily approachable. She has remained, and assures us that she will always remain, very approachable.

Channeling Popular Piety

The history of popular piety shows that devotion to Mary can become excessive if not checked—and unless religious leaders and liturgists are able to direct such devotions into approved forms of piety. The church hierarchy may not be able to control popular marian devotions effectively but it can channel them toward more legitimate forms of devotion. Devotions at Lourdes, for example, have been given a christocentric focus. Since the shrine was officially approved, the eucharistic celebration, the anointing of the sick, and the afternoon procession of the Blessed Sacrament have become highlights of the pilgrimage. Theologians ought to ask what deep human and spiritual needs are being met by such manifestations that seemingly are not being met by community liturgies or celebrations.

Any theological reshaping of the image of Mary must take into account the images of Mary in popular religious imagination.[21] Since all believers embrace some aspects of popular religion in their devotional life, popular piety will need a Mary who is a heavenly healer, intercessor, prophet, comforter, and friend. What theologians ignore, ordinary people will provide: apparition sites such as Lourdes, Fatima, and even Medjugorje will probably always be with us.

Suggestions for Further Reading

Elizondo, Virgil. "Mary and the Poor: A Model of Evangelizing Ecumenism," *Concilium* 168, pp. 59-64.

Turner, Victor and Edith. *Image and Pilgrimage in Christian Culture: Anthropological Perspectives.* New York: Columbia University Press, 1978.

NOTES

INTRODUCTION *"Didache" = teaching of the 12 apostles in the early Christian community*

1. Cited in John R. Shinners, "The Cult of Mary and Popular Belief," *Mary, Woman of Nazareth*, ed. Doris Donnelly (New York: Paulist Press, 1989), p. 163.

2. John McKenzie, "The Mother of Jesus in the New Testament," *Concilium* 168, ed. Hans Küng and Jürgen Moltmann (New York: Seabury, 1983), p. 9.

3. McKenzie, "The Mother of Jesus in the New Testament," p. 3.

4. Raymond E. Brown, Karl Donfried, Joseph Fitzmyer, and John Reumann, eds. *Mary in the New Testament* (Philadelphia: Fortress Press, 1978).

5. John Macquarrie, *Mary for All Christians* (London: William Collins & Sons, 1990).

6. John Paul II, *Redemptoris Mater* (1987), 48.

CHAPTER ONE

1. Norman Perrin, *The New Testament: An Introduction* (New York: Harcourt Brace Jovanovich, Inc., 1974), pp. 289-291.

2. "Journeying Together Towards the Third Millennium," Statement of the Federation of Asian Bishops, Bandung, Indonesia, July 27, 1990, in *For All the Peoples of Asia*, Gaudencio Rosales and Catalino Arevalo, eds., (Quezon City, Philippines: Claretian Press), 1992, 2.2.1.

3. Bertrand Buby, *Mary of Galilee: Mary in the New Testament* (New York: Alba House, 1994), p. 25.

4. See Brown et al., *Mary in the New Testament*, 41–44.

5. Joseph Grassi, *Mary, Mother & Disciple* (Wilmington, DE: Michael Glazier, 1988), p. 18.

6. Ivone Gebara and Maria Clara Bingemer, *Mary, Mother of God, Mother of the Poor* (Maryknoll, NY: Orbis Books), 1989, p.55.

7. Gebara and Bingemer, p. 56.

8. Raymond E. Brown, *Crises Facing the Church* (New York: Paulist Press, 1975), p. 92.

9. See Brown et al, *Mary in the New Testament*, pp. 117–119.

10. Anne Carr, "Mary, Model of Faith," in *Mary, Woman of Nazareth*, p. 16.

11. See Marina Warner, *Alone of All Her Sex: The Myth and Cult of the Virgin Mary* (New York: Vintage Books, 1983), pp. 68–78.

12. Donald Senior, "Gospel Portrait of Mary," in *Mary, Woman of Nazareth*, p. 104.

13. Richard Horsley, *The Liberation of Christmas: The Infancy Narratives in Social Context* (New York: Crossroad Publishing Co., 1989), p. 111.

14. Herman Hendrickx, *A Key to the Gospel of Luke* (Quezon City, Philippines: MST/Claretian Publications, 1992), p. 35.

15. See Edward Schillebeeckx, *Mary, Mother of the Redemption,* trans. N. D. Smith (New York: Sheed and Ward, 1964), pp. 144–145.

16. "Dogmatic Constitution on the Church," *The Documents of Vatican II*, ed. Walter Abbott (New York: Guild Press, 1966), 58; henceforth referred to as *Lumen Gentium*.

---

17. *Justice in the World*, Statement of the Synod of Bishops, (1974), 5.

18. Paul VI, *Evangelii Nuntiandi*, 18–19.

19. Brown et al., *Mary in the New Testament*, p. 6.

20. Grassi, pp. 71–75.

21. M. Girard, "La Composition Structurelle Des Septs Signes dans le Quatrième Evangile," *Sciences Religieuses* 9 (1980) 315–324, as cited in Grassi pp. 71–75. In the following discussion of the Johannine signs I rely heavily on Girard's restructuring of the seven signs.

22. Girard, cited in Grassi, p. 73.

23. Brown et al., *Mary in the New Testament*, p. 206.

24. Carr, "Mary, Model of Faith," in *Mary, Woman of Nazareth*, p. 21.

CHAPTER TWO

1. Rosemary Radford Ruether, *Mary, the Feminine Face of the Church* (Philadelphia: Westminster Press, 1977), p. 59.

2. Denzinger Schonmetzer, *Enchiridion Symbolorum Definitionum Declarationum.* See translation in *The Christian Faith,* eds. J. Neumer and J. Dupuis (London: Collins/Liturgical Press, 1983), 252. Henceforth referred to as DS.

3. DS, 148. See translation in *The Church Teaches*, eds. John F. Clarkson et al. (St. Louis: Herder Book Co., 1955), p. 172.

4. Gebara and Bingemer, p. 94.

5. *Redemptoris Mater*, 33.

6. *Redemptoris Mater*, 33.

7. Ruether, p. 60.

8. Raymond E. Brown, *The Virginal Conception and the Bodily Resurrection of Jesus* (London: Geoffrey Chapman, 1974), p. 28.

9. Bertrand Buby, *Mary, the Faithful Disciple* (New York: Paulist Press 1985), p. 55.

10. Brown et al., *Mary in the New Testament*, p. 114.

11. Brown et al., *Mary in the New Testament*, pp. 114–115.

12. Grassi, p. 69.

13. Grassi, p. 69.

14. Brown, *The Virginal Conception*, pp. 34–35.

15. *Encyclopedia of Catholicism*, gen ed. Richard McBrien (San Francisco: HarperSanFrancisco, 1995), s.v. "Virginity of Mary," Elizabeth Johnson.

16. Johnson, "Virginity of Mary," *Encyclopedia of Catholicism*, p. 837.

17. DS 503.

18. DS 1880.

19. Brown et al., *Mary in the New Testament*, pp. 120–121.

20. Brown et al., *Mary in the New Testament*, pp. 120–121.

21. Brown, *The Virginal Conception*, p. 66.

22. Brown et al., *Mary In the New Testament*, pp.124–125.

23. Karl Rahner, "Mary and the Christian Image of Woman," *Theological Investigations* XIX (New York: Crossroad Publishing Co., 1983), p. 211.

24. Leonardo Boff, *The Maternal Face of God* (San Francisco: Harper & Row, 1987), p. 141.

25. Joseph Komonchak, Mary Collins, and Dermot Lane, eds., *The New Dictionary of Theology* (Wilmington, DE: Michael Glazier, 1987), p. 535.

26. John L. McKenzie, "The Mother of Jesus in the New Testament," p. 7.

27. Rahner, "Courage for Devotion to Mary," *Theological Investigations,* Vol XIII (New York: Crossroad Publishing Co., 1992), p. 135.

28. See *The New Dictionary of Theology*, pp. 421–423.

29. See Elaine Pagels, *Adam, Eve, and the Serpent* (New York: Vintage Books, 1989), pp. 57–77.

30. Pagels, *Adam, Eve, and the Serpent,* pp. 64–65.

31. Grassi, p. 112.

32. Grassi, p. 112

33. Cited in W. J. Burghardt, "Mary in Western Patristic Thought," in J. B. Carol ed., *Mariology* (Milwaukee: Bruce Publishing Company, 1954), Vol I.

34. Epist, 63, N. 33.

35. *The Teachings of the Church Fathers,* ed. John R. Willis (New York: Herder and Herder, 1966), 781.

36. *The Teachings of the Church Fathers,* 786.

37. Brown, *The Virginal Conception,* p. 39.

38. Eric Neumann, *The Great Mother,* trans. Ralph Manheim (Princeton, NJ: Princeton University Press, 1963).

39. Bruce Malina, "From Isis to Medjugorje: Why Apparitions?" *Biblical Theology Bulletin,* 20:2 (Summer 1990).

CHAPTER THREE

1. The feast of the immaculate conception uses a conception of Jesus text (Luke 1:26–38) that pastorally confuses people into thinking it is a feast about the conception of Jesus.

2. Hilda Graef, *Mary, A History of Doctrine and Devotion,* Vol I (London: Sheed and Ward, 1963), pp. 45–46.

3. Graef, pp. 75–76.

4. Graef, p. 53.

5. Graef, p. 40.

6. Graef, pp. 41–42.

7. Herbert McCabe, "The Immaculate Conception," *Doctrine and Life,* 1975, pp. 871–872.

8. *Encyclopedia of Catholicism,* s.v. "Blessed Virgin Mary," Elizabeth Johnson, p. 834.

9. McCabe, p. 871.

10. Pius IX, *Ineffabilis Deus,* in DS 2803, *The Christian Faith in the Doctrinal Documents of the Catholic Church,* eds. J. Neuner and J. Dupuis, 709.

11. John Macquarrie, "Immaculate Conception," *Mary's Place in Christian Dialogue* (Wilton, CT: Morehouse–Barlow Co), p. 98.

12. Elaine Pagels, *Adam, Eve, and the Serpent* p. 99.

13. Gil Bailie, *Violence Unveiled: Humanity at the Crossroads* (New York: Crossroad Publishing Co., 1995).

14. Bailie, p. 207.

15. See Kathleen Coyle, "Original Sin: Residue of Some Primal Crime?" *East Asian Pastoral Review,* Vol 29, No 3, 1992, pp. 330–344. Also published in *Doctrine and Life,* Vol 43, February 1993, pp. 83–94. See also Sebastian Moore, *Let This Mind Be in You* (London: Darton, Longman & Todd, 1985).

16. Jonathan Schell, *The Fate of the Earth* (New York: Alfred E. Knopf, 1982), p. 67.

17. Walter T. Brennan, "The Issue of Archetypes," *Marianum* LII (1990), pp. 34–35. See the insightful discussion on archetypes in this article.

18. See William Shannon, "Original Blessing: The Gift of the True Self," *The Way,* January, 1990, pp. 37–46.

19. Cited in Shannon, p. 38.

20. Johnson, *Encyclopedia of Catholicism,* s.v. "Assumption of the Blessed Virgin," p. 104.

21. Pius XII, *Muntificentissimus Deus,* in *Acta Apostolicae Sedis* (1950), 42:757. See

English translation in *The Catholic Mind*, 65–78 (1951). Henceforth referred to as *MD*.

22. *MD*, 754.

23. *MD*, 758.

24. *Lumen Gentium*, 68.

25. *Lumen Gentium*, 68.

26. *Lumen Gentium*, 69.

27. Cited in Rosemary Ruether, *Sexism and God-Talk* (Boston: Beacon Press, 1983), p. 151.

CHAPTER FOUR

1. Graef, Vol I, p. 48.

2. Cited in Archimandrite Ephrem, "Mary in Eastern Church Literature," *The Month* August/September 1989, p. 315.

3. *Redemptoris Mater,* 31–32.

4. Graef, Vol I, pp. 50–55.

5. Graef, Vol I, p. 37. Graef notes that Justin may have received this parallelism as part of the postapostolic tradition when he was converted at Ephesus.

6. Graef, Vol I, p. 88.

7. Graef, Vol I, p. 182.

8. See Theodore Roszak, *Where the Wasteland Ends: Politics and Transcendence in Post-Industrial Society* (New York: Doubleday & Co., 1973).

9. Eleanor McLaughlin, "Equality of Souls, Inequality of Sexes: Woman in Medieval Theology," *Religion and Sexism,* ed. Rosemary R. Ruether (New York: Simon & Schuster, 1974), p. 246.

10. Elizabeth Johnson, "Marian Devotion in the Western Church," *Christian Spirituality: High Middle Ages and Reformation, An Encyclopedic History of the Religious Quest,* ed. Jill Raitt (New York: Crossroad Publishing Co., 1986), p. 411.

11. Carlos Eire, *War Against the Idols: The Reformation of Worship from Erasmus to Calvin* (London: CUP, 1986), pp. 11–12.

12. Eire, p. 14.

13. Cited in Graef, Vol II, p. 10.

14. Gottfried Maron, "Mary in Protestant Theology," *Concilium* 168, p. 41.

15. Charles Dickson, "Mariology: A Protestant Reconsideration," *American Ecclesiastical Review* (May 1974) pp. 306–307.

16. Graef, Vol II, p. 32.

17. Graef, Vol II, p. 57.

18. Graef, Vol II, p. 34.

19. Graef, Vol II, p. 35.

20. Graef, Vol II, p. 33.

21. Graef, Vol II, p. 75.

22. Rosemary Haughton, "There is Hope for a Tree," unpublished paper, p. 14.

23. Haughton, "There is Hope for a Tree," p. 15.

24. Gebara and Bingemer, p. 25.

25. Shinners, "The Cult of Mary and Popular Belief," *Mary, Woman of Nazareth,* p. 163.

26. Shinners, "The Cult of Mary and Popular Belief," *Mary, Woman of Nazareth,* p. 163.

27. See Anne Carr, *Transforming Grace* (San Francisco: Harper & Row, 1988), pp. 134–214, and Sallie McFague, *Metaphorical Theology: Models of God in Religious Language* (Philadelphia: Fortress Press, 1985), pp. 98–101.

28. Philippine Country Report on Women 1986–1995: Fourth World Conference on Women, Beijing, China, September 4–15, 1995, prepared by the National Commission on the Role of Filipino Women, in cooperation with the National Coordinating Commission for Beijing (Manila: NCRFW, 1995), p. 5.

29. Carr, "Mary in the Mystery of the Church," in *Mary According to Women,* ed. Carol Frances Jegen (Kansas City: Leaven Press, 1985), pp. 12–13.

CHAPTER FIVE

1. Pope Pius X, Encyclical Letter *Ad Deum Illum,* in *The Papal Encyclicals* 1803–1939 (A Consortium Book / McGrath Publishing Co., 1981), p. 14.

2. Quoted in Frederick M. Jelly, "Characteristics of Contemporary Mariology," *Chicago Studies,* Vol. 27, (1988).

3. *Lumen Gentium,* 54.

4. See Carr, "Mary in the Mystery of the Church," pp. 12–19.

5. Cited in Carr, "Mary in the Mystery of the Church," p. 12.

6. Carr, "Mary in the Mystery of the Church," p. 13.

7. Carr, "Mary in the Mystery of the Church," p. 12.

8. Cited in Carr, "Mary in the Mystery of the Church," p. 12.

9. *Lumen Gentium,* 53.

10. *Lumen Gentium,* 61

11. *Lumen Gentium,* 58.

12. *Lumen Gentium,* 62.

13. *Lumen Gentium,* 60.

14. Elizabeth Johnson, "Saints and Mary," *Systematic Theology: Roman Catholic Perspective,* eds. Francis S. Fiorenza and John P. Galvin (Dublin: Gill & Macmillan, 1992), p. 483.

15. Carr, "Mary in the Mystery of the Church," p. 15.

16. See Mary Hines, "Mary and the Prophetic Mission of the Church," *Journal of Ecumenical Studies,* 28:2 (Spring 1991).

17. *Lumen Gentium,* 53.

18. *Lumen Gentium,* 54.

19. *Redemptoris Mater,* 16.

20. Paul VI, *Marialis Cultus* (1974), Introduction.

21. *Marialis Cultus,* Introduction

22. *Marialis Cultus,* 36.

23. *Marialis Cultus,* 24.

24. *Marialis Cultus,* 37–38.

25. *Marialis Cultus,* 34.

26. *Marialis Cultus,* 34.

27. *Marialis Cultus,* 37.

28. *Marialis Cultus,* 37.

29. *Marialis Cultus,* 37.

30. *Redemptoris Mater,* 48.

31. *Redemptoris Mater,* 9.

32. *Redemptoris Mater,* 1.

33. *Redemptoris Mater,* 40.

34. *Redemptoris Mater,* 33.

35. *Redemptoris Mater,* 34.

36. *Redemptoris Mater,* 46.

37. *Redemptoris Mater,* 46.

38. U.S. Bishops Pastoral, *Behold Your Mother: Woman of Faith,* in *Catholic Mind,* 42 (1974), pp. 26–64.

39. *Behold Your Mother,* 142.

40. *Behold Your Mother,* 142.

CHAPTER SIX

1. See Elizabeth Johnson, "The Symbolic Character of Theological Statements about Mary," *Journal of Ecumenical Studies* 22:2 (Spring 1985), 312–335.

2. Sallie McFague, *Metaphorical Theology: Models of God in Religious Language* (Philadelphia: Fortress Press, 1987), p. 17.

3. Regina A. Coll, *Christianity and Feminism in Conversation* (Mystic, CT: Twenty–Third Publications, 1994), p. 38.

4. Stephen Happel, "Symbol," in *The New Dictionary of Theology*, p. 997. See also the very informative articles by Gerard A. Arbuckle, "Communicating through Symbols," *Human Development,* Vol 8, No 1, Spring 1987, and "Appreciating the Power of Myths," *Human Development,* Vol 8, No 4, Winter 1987.

5. Cited in Sallie McFague, *Models of God: Theology for an Ecumenical Nuclear Age,* (New York: Crossroad Publishing Co., 1981), p. 197.

6. Cited in Theodore Ross, "Catholicism and Fundamentalism," *New Theology Review,* Vol I, No 2 (May 1988), p. 75.

7. David Tracy, *The Analogical Imagination: Christian Theology and the Culture of Pluralism* (New York: Crossroad Publishing Co., 1981), p. 140.

8. Carr, "Mary, Model of Faith," *Mary, Woman of Nazareth,* p. 13.

9. McFague, *Models of God,* p. 20.

10. Cited in *Models of God,* p. 6.

11. Walter Burghardt, "Mary in Western Patristic Thought," *Mariology,* Vol I, ed. Juniper B. Carol (Milwaukee: Bruce Publishing, 1954), p. 109.

12. See Brown, "Hermeneutics," *The Jerome Biblical Commentary,* eds. Raymond Brown, Joseph Fitzmyer and Roland Murphy (Englewood: Prentice Hall, 1968), Nos. 80–81.

13. Ida Raming, "From the Freedom of the Gospel to the Petrified Men's Church: The Rise and Development of Male Domination in the Church," *Concilium* 134 (1980): 5.

14. Michael O'Carroll, *Theotokos: A Theological Encyclopedia of the Blessed Virgin Mary* (Dublin: Dominican Publications, 1982), p. 140.

15. Cited in Carol, Vol I, p. 111.

16. Carol, Vol I, p. 112.

17. Carol, Vol I, p. 112.

18. Carol, Vol I, p. 112.

19. Cited in Carol, Vol I, p. 122.

20. Cited in Kari Vogt,"'Becoming Male': One Aspect of an Early Christian Anthropology." *Concilium* 182, 78.

21. Cited in Mary Gordon, "Coming to Terms with Mary," *Commonweal* (January 25, 1982):11.

22. Kari Børresen, "Mary in Catholic Theology," *Concilium* 168, (1983): 51.

23. Carol, Vol I, p. 117.

24. J. Sprenger and H. Kramer, *Malleus Maleficarum,* trans. Montague Summers, pt 1, q. 6 (London: Pushkin Press, 1948).

25. *Lumen Gentium,* 56.

26. *Lumen Gentium,* 63.

27. John Paul II, *Mulieris Dignitatem,* 9.

28. Donal Flanagan, *The Theology of Mary* (Hales Corners, WI: Clergy Book Service, 1976), p. 97.

29. See studies on effects of Gnosticism on Christianity. Also footnote 25, Chapter 2.

30. Johnson, "Marian Tradition and the Reality of Women," *Horizons* 12/1 (1985): 123.

31. Johnson, "Marian Tradition and the Reality of Women," p. 124.

32. Elisabeth Schüssler Fiorenza, *In Memory of Her* (London: SCM Press, 1983), p. 287.

33. Fiorenza, *In Memory of Her,* p. 290.

34. Fiorenza, *In Memory of Her,* pp. 274–275.

35. See Anne Primavesi, *From Apocalypse to Genesis* (Minneapolis: Fortress Press, 1991), pp. 222–226.

36. Primavesi, p. 226.

37. Haughton, p. 14.

38. Ruether, *New Woman, New Earth* (New York: Seabury Press, 1975), p. 59.

CHAPTER SEVEN

1. Johnson, "Mary and the Image of God," *Mary, Woman of Nazareth,* p. 36.

2. For this and the following examples, see Johnson, "Mary and the Female Face of God," *Theological Studies* 50 (1989); p. 508.

3. Johnson, "Mary and the Female Face of God," p. 509.

4. Johnson, *She Who Is: The Mystery of God in Feminist Theological Discourse* (New York: Crossroad Publishing Co., 1992), p. 128.

5. ST I, q. 36, a.1, cited in *She Who Is,* p. 128.

6. Elsie Gibson, "Mary and the Protestant Mind," *Review for Religious* 24 (1965) 397.

7. Johnson, *She Who Is,* p. 142.

8. See for example Leonardo Boff, *Trinity and Society* (Maryknoll: Orbis Books, 1988), pp. 196–198.

9. Johnson, *She Who Is,* p. 54.

10. Johnson, *She Who Is,* p. 171.

11. Catherine La Cugna, *God for Us: The Trinity and the Holy Spirit* (San Francisco: Harper & Row, 1991), p. 1.

12. La Cugna, *God for Us,* p. 382.

13. La Cugna, *God for Us,* p. 366.

14. Rahner, p. 211.

15. Rahner, p. 213.

16. Rahner, p. 215.

17. Leonardo Boff and Clodovis Boff, *Introducing Liberation Theology* (Maryknoll: Orbis Books, 1987), p. 57.

18. Cited in Johnson, "Reconstructing a Theology of Mary," *Mary, Woman of Nazareth,* pp. 71–79.

19. See Boff, "Mary, Prophetic Woman of Liberation," *The Maternal Face of God,* trans. R. Barr and J. Dierksmeier (San Francisco: Harper & Row, 1987), pp. 188–203.

20. Boff, "Mary, Prophetic Woman of Liberation," p. 189.

21. *Third General Conference of Latin American Bishops* (Washington: National Conference of Catholic Bishops, 1979), p. 299.

22. Coll, p. 82.

23. Rahner, p. 217.

24. Hans Urs von Balthasar, *Elucidations* (London: SPCK, 1975), pp. 72–74.

25. Urs von Balthasar, pp 72–74

26. Johnson, "Saints and Mary," *Systematic Theology: Roman Catholic Perspective,* p. 487.

27. Bernard Lonergan, *Philosophy of God, and Theology: Relationship between Philosophy of God and the Fundamental Speciality, Systematics* (London: Darton, Longman & Todd, 1973), pp. 33–34.

28. Virginia Fabella and Mercy Oduyoye, *With Passion and Compassion* (New York: Orbis Books, 1988), p. 121.

29. *Marialis Cultus,* 35.

30. Gustavo Gutiérrez, *The God of Life,* trans. Matthew J. O'Connell (Maryknoll: Orbis Books, 1991), p. 179.

APPENDIX

1. Victor and Edith Turner, *Image and Pilgrimage in Christian Culture: Anthropological Perspectives* (New York: Columbia University Press, 1978), pp. 205–206.

2. Turner, p. 7.

3. One such list is offered by Sandra L. Zimdars-Swartz, *Encountering Mary: From La Salette to Medjugorje* (Princeton: Princeton University Press,1991), pp. 271-278.

4. *Behold Your Mother,* no 100.

5. Gebara and Bingemer, p. 148.

6. Gebara and Bingemer, p. 147.

7. Virgil Elizondo, "Mary and the Poor: A Model of Evangelizing Ecumenism," *Concilium* 168, p. 59.

8. Cited in "Apparitions of the Blessed Virgin," Mary Aquin O'Neill, *Encyclopedia of Catholicism*, Richard McBrien, gen. ed. (San Francisco: HarperSanFrancisco, 1995), p. 79.

9. O'Neill, "Apparitions of the Blessed Virgin," p. 79

10. Johnson, *Mary, Woman of Nazareth,* p. 41.

11. Michael O'Carroll, *Theotokos,* p. 47.

12. René Laurentin, *Lourdes,* p. 438, cited in Johnson.

13. Graef, Vol II, p. 103.

14. Schillebeeckx, *Mary Mother of the Redemption* (New York: Herder and Herder, 1964), p. 197.

15. Schillebeeckx, p. 197.

16. Carr, "Mary in the Mystery of the Church," in *Mary According to Women*, p. 9.

17. See footnote 5.

18. Barbara C. Pope, "Immaculate and Powerful," *Immaculate and Powerful: The Female in Social Image and Social Reality* ed., Clarissa Atkinson (Boston: Beacon Press, 1985), p. 195.

19. Turner, p. 236.

20. Shinners, p. 176.

21. For a study of popular religiosity in the context of Philippine culture, see Joe de Mesa, *In Solidarity with the Culture* (Quezon City: Maryhill School of Theology, 1987).

Selected Bibliography

ARTICLES

Bearsley, Patrick J. "Mary, the Perfect Disciple: A Paradigm for Mariology." *Theological Studies*, 1980, 461–504.

Brennan, Walter. "The Issue of Archetypes in Marian Devotion." *Marianum* LII (1990), p.1741.

_____. "Recent Developments in Marian Theology." *New Theology Review*, Vol 8, No 2, May, 1995, pp. 49–58.

Cummings, Owen. "Understanding the Immaculate Conception." *The Furrow*, December, 1979, pp. 767–771.

Haughton, Rosemary, "There is Hope for a Tree." Study Paper, unpublished.

Hines, Mary. "Mary and the Prophetic Mission of the Church." *Journal of Ecumenical Studies*, 28:2, Spring 1991, pp. 281–297.

Jelly, Frederick M. "Characteristics of Contemporary Mariology." *Chicago Studies,* Vol 27, 1988, pp. 63–79.

Johnson, Elizabeth. "Blessed Virgin Mary." *Encyclopedia of Catholicism*, Richard McBrien, gen. ed. (San Francisco: HarperSanFrancisco), 1995, pp. 832–838.

_____. "The Marian Tradition and the Reality of Women." *Horizons*, 12/1, 1985: 116–135.

_____."Mary and the Female Face of God." *Theological Studies*, 50/3, 1989: 500–526.

_____."Saints and Mary." in *Systematic Theology: Roman Catholic Perspectives* eds. Francis S. Fiorenza and John P. Galvin (Dublin: Gill & Macmillan), 1992, pp. 467–501.

Malina, Bruce. "Mother And Son"; "From Isis to Medjugorje: Why Apparitions?" *Biblical Theology Bulletin, Mutuality vs Complementarity: New Mariological Challenge*, Vol 20, Summer 1990, No 2, 46–94. The entire issue is devoted to Mary.

McCabe, Herbert. "The Immaculate Conception." *Doctrine & Life*, Dublin: Dominican Publications, December 1975, pp. 869–771.

BOOKS

Anderson, H. G., Stafford, J. F., and Burgess, J. A., eds. *The One Mediator, the Saints, and Mary.* Minneapolis: Augsburg Press, 1992.

Atkinson, Clarissa, ed. *Immaculate and Powerful: The Female in Social Image and Social Reality.* Boston: Beacon Press, 1985.

Bailie, Gil. *Violence Unveiled: Humanity at the Crossroads.* New York: Crossroad, 1995.

Boff, Leonardo. *The Maternal Face of God.* San Francisco, Harper & Row, 1987.

Brown, Raymond. *The Birth of the Messiah*. New York: Image Books, 1979.

_____. *Crises Facing the Church*. London, Darton, Longman & Todd Ltd, 1975.

_____. *The Virginal Conception and Bodily Resurrection of Jesus*. New York, Paulist, 1973.

Brown, R.E., Donfried, K.P., Fitzmyer, J.A., Reumann, J., eds. *Mary in the New Testament*. Philadelphia: Fortress Press, 1978.

Buby, Bertrand. *Mary of Galilee*. New York: Alba House, 1994.

Carol, J.B. *Mariology*, 2 Vols. Milwaukee, Bruce Publishing Co, 1955.

Carr, Anne. *Transforming Grace*. San Francisco: Harper & Row, 1988.

Coll, Regina A. *Christianity and Feminism in Conversation*. Mystic, CT: Twenty-Third Publications, 1994.

Conn, Joann Wolski, ed. *Women's Spirituality*. New York: Paulist Press, 1986.

Donnelly, Doris, ed. *Mary, Woman of Nazareth*. New York: Paulist Press, 1990.

Fabella, Virginia and Oduyoye, Mercy, eds. *With Passion and Compassion*. New York: Orbis Books, 1988.

Flanagan, Donal. *The Theology of Mary*. Hales Corners, Wisconsin: Clergy Book Service, 1976.

Gebara, Ivone, Maria C. Bingemer. *Mary, Mother of God, Mother of the Poor*. Maryknoll, NY: Orbis Books, 1989.

Graef, Hilda. *Mary: A History of Doctrine and Devotion*, 2 Vols. New York, Sheed & Ward, 1965.

Grey, Mary. *Feminism Redemption and the Christian Tradition*. Mystic, CT: Twenty-Third Publications, 1990.

Grassi, Joseph. *Mary, Mother & Disciple*. Wilmington, DE: Michael Glazier, 1988.

Hendrickx, Herman. *A Key to the Gospel of Luke*. Quezon City, Philippines: MST/Claretian Publications, 1992.

Horsley, Richard A. *The Liberation of Christmas: The Infancy Narratives in Social Context*. New York: Crossroad Publishing, 1989.

Jegen, Carol Frances, ed. *Mary According to Women*. Kansas City: Leaven Press, 1985.

Johnson, Elizabeth. *She Who Is: The Mystery of God in Feminist Theological Discourse*. New York: Crossroad Publishing, 1992.

_____. "Marian Devotion in the Western Church." *Christian Spirituality: High Middle Ages and Reformation*, ed. Jill Raitt. New York: Crossroad Publishing, 1988, pp. 392–440.

_____. "Saints and Mary." *Systematic Theology: Roman Catholic Perspective*. Eds., F. Fiorenza and J. Galvin. Dublin: Gill & Macmillan, 1992.

John Paul II. *Redemptoris Mater*. Manila, St. Paul Publications, 1987.

Küng, H., and J. Moltmann, eds. *Concilium 168*. New York: Seabury Press, 1983.

LaCugna, Catherine M. "God in Communion With Us." *Freeing Theology: The Essentials of Theology in Feminist Perspective*, ed. Catherine M. LaCugna. San Francisco: HarperSanFrancisco, 1993, p. 83–114.

_____. *God for Us: The Trinity and Christian Life*. San Francisco: HarperSanFrancisco, 1991.

Maquarrie, John. *Mary for All Christians*. London: Collins & Sons, 1990.

Neumann, Eric. *The Great Mother*. trans. Ralph Manheim. Princeton, NJ: Princeton University Press, 1955.

McFague, Sallie. *Models of God*. Philadelphia: Fortress Press, 1987.

Neumann, Eric. *The Great Mother*. trans. Ralph Manheim. Princeton, NJ: Princeton University Press, 1955.

McFague, Sallie. *Models of God*. Philadelphia: Fortress Press, 1987.

O'Carroll, Michael. *Theotokos: A Theological Encyclopedia of the Blessed Virgin Mary*, rev. ed. Dublin: Dominican Publications, 1983.

O'Donnell, Christopher. *At Worship with Mary*. Wilmington, DE: Michael Glazier, 1988.

Paul VI. *Marialis Cultus*. Manila: Paulist Press, 1974.

Rahner, Karl. "Mary and the Christian Image of Woman." *Theological Investigations* Vol XIX. New York: Crossroad Publishing, 1983.

Ruether, Rosemary Radford. *Sexism and God-Talk*. Boston: Beacon Press, 1983.

_____. *Mary, the Feminine Face of the Church*. Philadelphia: Westminster Press, 1977.

_____, ed. *Religion and Sexism*. New York: Simon & Schuster, 1974.

Thompson, William M. *Christology and Spirituality*. New York: Crossroad Publishing, 1991.

Turner, Victor and Edith. *Image and Pilgrimage in Christian Culture*. New York: Columbia University Press, 1978.

Warner, Marina. *Alone of All Her Sex*. New York: Vintage Books, 1983.

Zimdars-Swartz, Sandra L. *Encountering Mary: From La Salette to Medjugorje*. Princeton, NJ: Princeton University Press, 1991.

INDEX

Of Related Interest ...

The Hope for Wholeness
A Spirituality for Feminists
Katherine Zappone
The author maps out a clear path, one that points to the necessity of find-ing a wholeness that all—women and men alike—can embrace. She con-cludes that investigating the various feminist spiritualities will transform this wholeness from a hope to a reality.

ISBN: 0-89622-495-3, 195 pp, $12.95

Feminism, Redemption and the Christian Tradition
Mary Grey
Based on the belief that within Christian tradition there is a liberating dream to be recovered, this book poses the argument that to reclaim this dream, women must recover a positive sense of self that can ultimately lead to a new experience of redemption.

ISBN: 0-89622-428-7, 250 pp, $16.95

The Christology of Rosemary Radford Ruether
A Critical Introduction
Mary Hembrow Snyder
Readers are introduced to the forceful ideas, widespread community and political involvement, and far-reaching religious theory of Ruether. The book explores the implications of Ruether's theology for ecumenism, spiri-tuality, soteriology, theological method and the church's self-understanding.

ISBN: 0-89622-358-2, 152 pp, $12.95

In Search of the Christ-Sophia
Jann Aldredge-Clanton
The author presents an inclusive christology based on the biblical parallel between Christ and Sophia (Wisdom) that will help Christians expand their horizons and rethink traditional beliefs. This book combines theological scholarship with pastoral sensitivity to demonstrate that a christology inclu-sive of both male and female images is vital to a liberating, egalitarian church.

ISBN: 0-89622-629-8, 192 pp, $14.95

Available at religious bookstores or from

TWENTY-THIRD PUBLICATIONS
XXIII P.O. Box 180 • Mystic, CT 06355 • 1-800-321-0411